IT'S ALMOST TOO MUCH TO FACE FOR—

THOMAS CARDIF—Rhodan's son, who assumes the role of his father

REGINALD BELL—Rhodan's First Deputy. He comes close to taking over

Allan D. Mercant—the Solar Marshal suspects Rhodan of . . . *murder!*

Homunk—the Wonder Robot wonders

"IT"—the Master of Wanderer is vastly amused

John Marshall, Fellmer Lloyd & Pucky—the *Mutants* see a phantom behind the mask

Brazo Alkher & Stant Nolinov—Solar Fleet officers accused of treason

Banavol—the Arkonide is a catspaw

A-Thol—an Anti in disguise

Rhobal—the High Priest of Baalol seeks immortality

Catepan—a Springer patriarch

Dr. Pinter—Doctor in charge of the *Ironduke* clinic

Maj. Lyon—A chart room officer of the *Ironduke*

Jac Hannibal—Specialist in hypercom equipment aboard the *Ironduke*

Fut-Gii—the ghost of a galactic trader

. . . and the spaceships *Wellington, Baa-Lo & Ironduke*

RHODAN'S SON FACES A CRISIS

PERRY RHODAN: Peacelord of the Universe

Series and characters created and directed by Karl-Herbert Scheer and Walter Ernsting.

ACE BOOKS EDITION

Managing Editor: FORREST J ACKERMAN

WENDAYNE ACKERMAN
 Translater-in-Chief
 & Series Coordinator

CHARLES VOLPE
 Art Director

PAT LOBRUTTO
 Editor

Sig Wahrman
Stuart J. Byrne
 Associate Translators

Perry Rhodan

104

THE MAN WITH TWO FACES

by Kurt Brand

ace books
A Division of Charter Communications Inc.
A GROSSET & DUNLAP COMPANY
1120 Avenue of the Americas
New York, New York 10036

THE MAN WITH TWO FACES

Copyright © 1976 by Ace Books

An Ace Book by arrangement with
Arthur Moewig Verlag

All Rights Reserved

TIME VAULT: "The Impossible Highway" copyright © 1940 for *Thrilling Wonder Stories;* a check in payment has been sent to the author's widow. Illustration for "The Impossible Highway" by FRANK R. PAUL; a check is being held for his widow or daughter by the representative of the Estate.* "The Face in the Mask", copyright © 1961 for *Fantastic Stories of Imagination;* reprinted by arrangement with the author's agent*

TRIPLANETARY AGENT: Copyright © 1976 by William B. Ellern; by arrangement with the author's agent*

*Forrest J Ackerman, 2495 Glendower Ave., Hollywood/CA 90027

This Issue Dedicated To
G. PEYTON WERTENBAKER
Only 5 Stories
But All Memorable—
Elaine's Tomb
The Chamber of Life
The Coming of the Ice
The Man from the Atom
The Ship That Turned Aside
—Evergreen Stories by the
Author Eventually Known as
Green Peyton

First Ace Printing: October 1976

Printed in U.S.A.

HERE'S HOW IT HAPPENS

STARDUST EDITORIAL
"Across the Seas of Space"
Wendayne Ackerman
page 7

Prolog
page 13

1/ GALACTIC ENEMY #1
page 15

2/ THE EXTORTIONIST
page 38

3/ WHEN "IT" LAUGHED
page 64

4/ LONG ARM OF BAALOL
page 86

5/ DAY OF THE ANTI-RHODAN
page 109

THE SHIP OF THINGS TO COME
"Wonderflower of Utik"
By Kurt Mahr
page 131

THE TIME VAULT
"The Face in the Mask"
Estelle Frye
page 132

SMITHIAN SERIAL
"Triplanetary Agent" Pt. 5
William B. Ellern
page 145

SON OF TIME VAULT
"The Impossible Highway"
Oscar J. Friend
page 16

THE PERRYSCOPE
Various Voice
page 182

DARKON'S CORNER
Let's Face It
page 187

> **STARDUST EDITORIAL**
> "Across the Seas of Space"
> By
> Wendayne Ackerman

German PERRY RHODAN readers, who are light-years ahead of us in the universe-spanning saga of our favorite science fiction serial, are most eager to establish contact with their American counterparts. What better way of furthering understanding between the nations of this world than sharing enthusiasms and curiosity about what life on other planets, in other galaxies or in our own future might be like; than discussing it with friends on this side as well as the other side of the ocean? So here is your chance to exchange letters, fanzines, books, etc. with the following German fans who have requested me to get them in touch with our PERRY RHODAN readers.

Perry Rhodan Club PALADIN informs me:

Dear Mrs. Ackerman,

We have seen your address in the Perry Rhodan Yearbook 1976. We would like to contact American Perry Rhodan Clubs and we hope you will be able to assist us in this matter. Our address is:

PRC PALADIN c/o Peter Scharle
D-4175 Wachtendank 1
Geneng 41, W. Germany

THE MAN WITH TWO FACES

Here are some excerpts of a long and interesting letter which by the way was the first I received as a result of an article about American Fandom which appeared last Spring in the German Perry Rhodan Yearbook 1976. Roland Rosenbauer not only writes a good letter but also good science fiction short stories. He had several published in the German equivalent of our own Shock Shorts. One of these has been translated into English and we hope you will be able to read it in the near future in the pages of our own magabook.

Roland likes the idea expressed in the previously mentioned article that American Fandom's activities should not be limited to the USA but should expand its horizons to include all Terra. Roland is a student, 20 years of age, president of PRClub "Thunderbolts", named after the Siganese Thunderbolt team, still to appear in the series. Roland is interested in music, works as a disk jockey in his spare time, builds airplane models, hopes to become a science fiction writer. His address:

Roland Rosenbauer
Markgraf-Alexanderstrasse 19
8501 Cadolzburg, W. Germany

Klaas Schaefer
Dorfstrasse 72
2981 Ostermoordorf
Ostfriesland, W. Germany

He is 16 years old, has a good knowledge of the English language. He would like to correspond with an American Perry Rhodan fan.

THE MAN WITH TWO FACES

Urs Schmidiger
Ebenaustrasse 5
CH-6048 HORW
Switzerland

Urs has studied English for 3 years in a high school in Luzern, a beautiful city in the German-speaking part of Switzerland and feels confident of discussing in English Perry Rhodan as well as other science fiction books.

He is interested also in the marginal areas of science & sport, particularly in basketball. He would like to meet a science fiction buff his age, 17-18 years old.

Christof Schuchert
Forsthausstrasse 19
6400 Fulda-Lehnerz, W. Germany

Christof owns several hundred German PERRY RHODAN books, is 17 years of age. He would like to correspond with an American girl; of course, only Perry Rhodan fans need apply! It would help if she'd have some knowledge of the German language too.

Michael Schurmann
Weiherstrasse 6
593 Siegen Weidenau, W. Germany

Michael is a true collector. He has not only the first edition of the German PERRY RHODAN series but also the second and an almost complete set of the third edition. He would be not averse in trading some German "Hefte" for the English language version. So here is your chance, American completists!

THE MAN WITH TWO FACES

Gerhard Schwan
5241 Scheuerfeld/Sieg
Zur Hell 3, W. Germany

He seems to be a fan of beautiful special editions of postage stamps, judging by the dazzling array of stamps on his letter addressed to me. He, too, seeks not only a penpal of his age, about 17-18 years, but also would like to have and trade, I guess, some American magabooks.

Joerg Staesche
Poetjerweg 37
282 Bremen 71, W. Germany

Joerg writes German but is able to read & understand English letters. This means he would like to find an American PERRY RHODAN enthusiast who will write to him in English but who on the other hand will have to be able to understand his German replies.

Lutzian Stephan
Bodenbacher Ring 91
322 Salzgitter 21, W. Germany

Lutzian would appreciate getting in touch with an American PERRY RHODAN fan club or PERRY RHODAN readers.

Rainer Stuetzel c/o Sawade
An der Fliesch 11
4100 Duisburg 25, W. Germany

Rainer writes a short letter in English which follows verbatim:

Dear Mrs. Ackermann

I'm a German Perry Rhodan-fan and I want to be in

correspondation with an American fan of this S.F.-serie. Please send me an address of an American fan.

Thank you
Yours
Rainer Stuetzel

Of course I cannot send him or the many other German PERRY RHODAN fans who wrote to me in response to the article about American PERRY RHODAN Fandom in the German PERRY RHODAN Yearbook 1976 any individual addresses of American fans. This has to come directly from you, the readers of our English language version, which I together with some helpers have been translating now for 8 years.

Prolog

It all came about because the intelligence organizations of both the Solar and Arkonide Imperiums had paid too little attention to the activities of the Antis. And so it was that the servants of Baalol were practically unhindered in carrying out their infamous 10-year plan, which was to distribute a deadly narcotic elixir called Liquitiv thruout the inhabited worlds of the galaxy.

But the custodians of interstellar Law & Order were not fundamentally to blame for being somewhat lax in their surveillance. After all, even the most outstanding scientists had formed the opinion that Liquitiv was eminently suitable for delaying the natural aging process of the human organism and that those who used the liqueur would experience a new vigor and muscle tone.

Their disastrous error has been discovered in the meantime and every effort is being made to cure the victims of the addiction.

However, what nobody has yet realized—not even the mutants—is something that can have an even heavier impact upon the destinies of all colonized worlds: Perry Rhodan is being held prisoner and at the helm is—

THE MAN WITH TWO FACES!

1/ GALACTIC ENEMY #1

TERRIBLY WRONG.

Something was terribly wrong and Reginald Bell couldn't quite put his finger on it. He shook his head in troubled thought as he laid the report aside. The document bore Perry Rhodan's signature. It was one of many that Bell had read this very day. All these documents had come to his desk directly from Rhodan's office. Some of them included Perry's handwritten comment: *approved*.

The same comment was on the report he was shaking his head about now: *Examination of the proposal of the Galactic Traders to establish an additional 300 trading posts within sovereign territory of the Solar Imperium.* The experts who had prepared the report had arrived at the unanimous opinion that the Springers' proposal should be rejected. But Rhodan had written his comment at the bottom of it: *These trading settlements are to be sanctioned. Signed: Rhodan.*

Bell sighed heavily. "Perry, Perry, what the devil's come over you since we've come back from Okul?"

Suddenly his temper got the best of him. He had to blow off steam by cursing aloud. Then he reached out to his button board and depressed the intercom switch.

Allan D. Mercant's face appeared on the videoscreen. When the Chief of Solar Intelligence saw Bell's fierce expression it told him all he needed to know for the moment. Mercant waited for Bell to speak his mind. It didn't look like very good news. Within 2 months after

THE MAN WITH TWO FACES

Rhodan had been brought back from Okul, wounded and in a deep state of mental shock, even laughter had become a thing of the past in his vicinity.

In his exasperation Bell blasted out: "Mercant, I've just gotten the input from the experts—you know, about the proposal for letting the star gypsies spread out farther into our own backyard. You know what Rhodan's written here? He says those Rippers* can go ahead and set up their tents! Now how does *that* grab you?"

To which Mercant calmly replied: "Well, if it keeps on going at this rate, unfortunately I'm going to be forced to increase Inelligence personnel by about 10 times their present strength."

"Then tell him that, Mercant!" shouted Bell.

Mercant begged off with a slight shaking of the head. "The Chief has become a man of solitary decisions, Bell."

*Ripoff Artists

THE MAN WITH TWO FACES

"So what's it all going to come to, Mercant? The more time goes by, the stranger Perry becomes to me—like he'd been hooked on Liquitiv! He acts spooked out** or something. I don't know. He never smiles anymore —not a trace of humor left in him. Everybody keeps out of his way, even Pucky."

"Maybe that's the crux of the matter. Maybe we're making it too obvious to him that he's become strange to us. Could be that our reaction to him is the very thing that drives him further into his isolation."

"Oh, butterfly pie***, Mercant! If he's headsick, so let him take a vacation, but let's not have these stellar pirates take over our whole back lot!"

"Face it, Mr. Bell—you're his closest friend," Mercant reminded him. "It's your duty to indicate this to the Chief."

"No way!" Bell exclaimed hotly. "Look, I've had to swallow some rough head-knockings already from the medicos. They leaned on me because I was giving Perry a bad time. Those drug-pluggers**** are after me all the time to lay off. They keep telling me to remember he's under shock therapy and that I shouldn't hock the rocket***** when they're trying to bring him thru his convalescence. But somebody's going to have to get to him when he makes wrong decisions. From all appearances I'm the worst candidate in the bullpen for that. But Mercant, you're much more of a diplomat than I am. Now why don't you drop by my office and pick up this proposal decision. Take it back in to Rhodan. I hope

---
**Spaced Out
***Horsefeathers, Balloon Juice, Baloney, Utter Nonsense
****Pill-Pushers
*****Rock The Boat

THE MAN WITH TWO FACES

he'll listen to you and stop this Springer invasion before it becomes a fact."

He noted Mercant's hesitation but didn't press him further. Allan D. Mercant was not a man who could be pushed. The decision had to come from himself.

"Alright," Mercant said finally. "I'll give it a try. You may expect me in 10 minutes, Mr. Bell."

"Great!" As Bell cut off the connection he uttered a heartfelt sigh of relief. But his concern for Rhodan remained.

Things had started to go wrong from the time Rhodan had decided on Okul to face his son Thomas Cardif alone. When they finally picked him up again he was wounded and almost out of his head. They had made a high-speed emergency flight with him back to Earth in order to get him into the hands of the doctors.

The greatest medical authorities had rushed to Rhodan's bedside and all their diagnoses were amazingly in common accord. The panel of experts also agreed very quickly on the best method of treatment for him. This was the Thmasson shock method, a therapy jointly developed by Terran and Ara doctors which minimized the intensity of deep mental disturbances so that when the course of treatment was over with the patient would recall it only as a vague dream.

After that the recovery process had moved forward with amazing swiftness in Rhodan's case. Only 3 days after application of the Thmasson therapy the authorities were able to announce: *Perry Rhodan, Administrator of the Solar Imperium, is on his way to recovery. He has passed all critical danger. No further bulletins will be issued.*

Within the stellar empire of Terra, Rhodan's illness

THE MAN WITH TWO FACES

had only generated sporadic concern here and there. Everything was overshadowed by the Liquitiv crisis and the millions of raving addicts. While the administrative staff in Terrania was still worrying about Rhodan's mental health, new large shipments of Liquitiv were brought into the Solar Imperium for the firsttime since the depletion caused by the blockade. This supply was sufficient to return the raging addicts to an apparent state of normalcy. In conjunction with this, however, the most gigantic preparations were being made both in Earth-controlled regions and in the Akron Imperium to complete an effort in only a few weeks which would provide massive production plants for generating sufficient quantities of the addition-healing Allitiv.

Rhodan had been released from the clinic in Terrania for some time already when it became known that all addicts would have him to thank if Allitiv succeeded in curing them of their narcotic addiction. At no time in the history of the Solar Imperium had Rhodan's star gleamed so brightly in the firmament of popularity as during those weeks of new rising hope.

And never before had any man been so accursed as Thomas Cardif. The Arkon worlds as well as the inhabitants of the Sol System knew the role that this man had played. A Universal search was being made for him; of course he was seen everywhere but whenever the clues were followed up they always led nowhere. Thomas Cardif appeared to be hiding out somewhere in the star jungle—in unexplored regions of the galaxy.

No one had guessed the actual truth!

No one could imagine that this man who was being sought by millions was in Terrania. Thomas Cardif had taken over the role of Perry Rhodan! Nobody knew that

THE MAN WITH TWO FACES

Perry Rhodan had been kidnaped and was now in the clutches of the Antis.

But the man who represented himself as Rhodan realized more and more each day what a risky game of roulette he was playing. The danger wasn't so much with the mutants whom he had feared so much at first. With them he used a double brain faculty which enabled him to simulate Rhodan's brainwave patterns whenever he knew that a telepathic or tracer mutant was around. This fact eliminated even the slightest suspicion that he could be taken for Thomas Cardif.

No. The danger of discovery lay in an entirely different area. Altho he had absorbed most of his father's knowledge, he did not possess the full magnitude of that intuition which had made Rhodan stand out from the masses of men.

Prof. Kalup was the first to get suspicious when he went into discussions with Cardif-Rhodan over development work concerning the linear space-drive. The scientist had stopped him in the middle of a statement to look at him incredulously. "Sir," he asked him, "where did you get such an idea as that?"

So Cardif-Rhodan had no alternative than to fall back on the Thmasson shock therapy as an excuse for extricating himself at the moment.

The Thmasson shock spectre seemed to cast its shadow over Terrania from then on. The man presumed to be Rhodan was seen far less frequently in the company of scientists, engineers or technicians. Ever since his return from Okul he had not manifested a single electrifying idea that might serve to rescue some stagnating project and drive it forward.

All the time it was something like: "The Chief doesn't

THE MAN WITH TWO FACES

have the old flash touch for technical problems—but it's because of the Thmasson shock therapy." Cardif had quickly learned to capitalize on that one perfect excuse.

With cool premeditation he had gone to his physicians and pointed out what had happened in his discussion with Prof. Kalup, even emphasizing his lapse of competence. "Is it possible," he asked them in mock concern, "that the Thmasson shock treatments have robbed me of some of my former thinking capacity?"

The doctors could not give yea or nay to the question. With a great inner sense of satisfaction he had left them with that to contemplate. So all dangers of this nature were always avoidable henceforth by his pretense of still being under the effects of the therapy.

In the public eye, however, he had not changed. Cardif was too much like his father, not only in outward appearance but also in many intellectual respects. In addition the knowledge he had taken over from him came in handy and with his own talents combined he had been able to make such a clever use of these assets that often he would appear to be Perry Rhodan to his father's closest friends.

But when he was alone—and from week to week he shut himself off more and more—then a real spectre would arise to haunt him. He was overcome by the increasing awareness of being a puppet in the hands of the Antis. They held the real Rhodan as their trump card and if he, Cardif, failed to dance to their tune they might put the thumb-screws to him.

Even at night he hardly slept any more.

In desperation he sought for a way to become independent of the Baalol cult. The longer he played Rhodan's role the more he was gripped by a sense of power

THE MAN WITH TWO FACES

and this new intoxication was serving to push his former hatred of his father more and more into the background. But he had also seen even this danger. Like one addicted he fought against the narcotic of power. He must not let it control him because one thing he'd been certain of from the very first minute: he could only operate as Cardif but never as Perry Rhodan.

The transference on Okul had only been a partial success. He attributed it to the limited time at his disposal, never suspecting that the cause of it lay within himself. The egoic "I" in Thomas Cardif was simply not capable of being subordinated in this pressing situation.

He heard someone knocking. "Yes?" he called out, startled. He was brought back to reality from the depths of brooding. By the time he looked toward the door he had collected himself. "Oh it's you, Mercant," he said as he saw his visitor enter. "I don't seem to recall putting you on the calendar for any discussion just now."

Formerly Perry Rhodan had spoken sharply like this once in awhile but only when justified. Since his return from Okul this tone was almost habitual with him.

The Solar Marshal did not allow himself to be intimidated or frightened away. He simply walked right in and took his customary seat to the left of Rhodan's desk. He spread out the experts' report and began. "Sir, I found this proposal study in Mr. Bell's office. May I bring to your attention the fact that the manpower strength of Solar Intelligence will have to be increased many times if 300 additional trade settlements are to be opened in the colonial territory of the Solar Imperium, on top of the many commercial bases the Galactic Traders already have there?"

Cardif-Rhodan's gray eyes held unwaveringly on Mer-

THE MAN WITH TWO FACES

cant's face. His sharply-chiseled features revealed nothing of his train of thought. Thomas Cardif was thinking at this moment of the Antis and was cursing them mentally. It was due to pressure from them that he had approved the proposal of the Galactic Traders. He was a victim of heir first attempt at extortion! Four days ago they had given him unmistakable signals by way of a Trader delegation that they would be able to judge his comportment accordingly if a negative decision was reached with regard to the trading post proposal.

The Springer patriarch who had brought him this message had not suspected exactly *what* he was transmitting to the First Administrator. But Cardif-Rhodan had perceived what was behind the hearty greetings. The name Fut-gli told him enough. Fut-gli had sent him greetings! But Fut-gli had been done away with 4 years ago while working for the Antis because as a Galactic Trader he had not been willing to wear the yoke of service to the Baalol priests.

And now here was Mercant who was trying to convince him to revoke his authorization of the proposal.

"Anything else, Mercant?" he asked coldly.

The Solar Marshal was clearly amazed. He stared at the man who to him was his Chief. "Sir," he stammered —and for him confusion was rare—"this can be a matter of life and death to use, expanding the already large number of alien settlements by another 300. We are simply not in in a position to keep an eye on all these Springer counting houses in the Solar Imperium—not to the extent that our security demands. We're opening our gates for a Trojan Horse!"

"You let me worry about that, Mercant! I have approved the proposal. Isn't that enough?"

THE MAN WITH TWO FACES

Inwardly, Thomas Cardif was highly agitated. He could well understand the Chief of Solar Intelligence. He also recognized what lay hidden behind the Springer proposal: a surreptitious takeover of the Solar Imperium by the Galactic Traders, with the priests of Baalol looming right behind them.

Mercant's face became a mask. His lips pressed together. Slowly, almost reluctantly, he gathered the report together and placed it in his portfolio. He nodded wordlessly to the Chief and got up and left.

Cardif's eyes followed him to the door. When it closed behind Mercant, he took a long deep breath. He clenched his fists in a helpless rage. "You Antis!" he muttered between his teeth. Then he was slightly startled when the videophone screen flickered to life.

Reginald Bell was calling him. He couldn't know yet that Mercant's visit had been unsuccessful. "Perry," he said, "Reception just informed me that you're ready to receive an Arkonide by the name of Banavol. Would you mind telling me what this man wants from us?"

Cardif was repeatedly irritated that Bell's curiosity kept mixing into his private affairs. He had often attempted to cut him out of such matters but every barb of innuendo had shattered against Bell's thick insensitivity. He wouldn't let go of the reins, it seemed, and against Cardif-Rhodan's most strenuous objections he managed to put up his own brand of argument: "Perry, as long as you're not 100% fit yet, I'll keep an eye on you. I owe you that and someday you'll thank me for it. I'll be damned if this Thmasson shock business hasn't turned you into a stranger to all of us! But do you get my point?"

Thomas Cardif had gotten the point, which he re-

THE MAN WITH TWO FACES

membered now while Bell was questioning him. However, he was not at a loss for a plausible answer. "My thick friend, it happens that Benavol's visit has to do with Thomas Cardif. Does that satisfy you?"

No. Reggie Bell was not at all satisfied. He was too well acquainted with the Arkonide mentality. In his opinion they were the biggest donks in the galaxy. Nor was he loathe to express that opinion now. "So when Solar Intelligence is beating its head against a blank wall, you think an Arkonide, of all people, can help us? OK, that's fine if you're not hurting for time. So you're really going to see him, Perry?"

Altho Cardif was inwardly resentful of Bell's stubbornness he attempted a touch of levity. "Yes, Fatso, I'd like to. It's nice that you've given your blessing. Anything else?"

Bell seemed to swell visibly with sudden impatience. "Yes, Perry, one thing more. Will you kick that habit of saying 'anything else?' You know it was bad enough before when you used that brushoff about 10 times a month but now it's a broken record—about 10 times a day! So try to knock it off, will you, old *sock*?"

"Yes, nurse," replied Cardif, attempting a sarcastic smile. "Thanks for the tip!"

* * * *

Bell chuckled slightly as he cut off the connection. Maybe Perry's recovery was making some progress after all, he thought. Once in awhile he cracked a smile at least.

When Mercant came in, Bell didn't need to ask any questions. The answer was written clearly on the Solar

THE MAN WITH TWO FACES

Marshal's rigid face as he tossed his portfolio onto Bell's desk. "The invasion is on!" he reported.

"You're kidding!"

"Am I?" retorted Mercant wearily.

"What reason did he come up with this time, Mercant?"

"Nowadays who gets any reasons from him?" Mercant replied. So what happens now, Bell?"

"Allan, how much preparation time do you need for beefing up the personnel in your outfit?"

Mercant waved his arms in a gesture of futility. "What do you mean, beef it up?" he protested. "I don't know of a hundred extra good men I could scare up, let alone 2000 of them! Mr. Bell, you know even the Intelligence service is something that has to be learned. I'll tell you this now so that there'll be no misunderstanding between the two of us: if another 300 Springer trading posts are set up in addition to what we're faced with already, that will overtax the capacity of Solar Intelligence to handle its job. And before that happens I'll apply for my pension!"

For once Bell controlled himself. "Mercant, I'm going to take a long chance. What I have in mind I'm telling you strictly in confidence. I'm going to make a slight amendment to that proposal—to the effect that only 100 new Springer camps will be allowed inside the Solar Imperium in any one year. That way you won't be faced with an invasion. It'll take those con artists 3 years to to make full use of the agreement. So on that basis are you still going to apply for your pension?"

"Mr. Bell, if you can do that . . ." Mercant's eyes had lighted up for a moment but then the hope faded. "If the Chief gets wind of it he'll quash the whole thing."

THE MAN WITH TWO FACES

"I'll worry about that if it happens, Mercant. By the way, do you know who's with th Chief at the moment? He's an Arkonide and he's here on Thomas Cardif business!"

"Do you know his name?" asked Mercant, not overly surprised.

"Banavol."

"He's known. Arkonide mother, Arkonide father; very alert, extremely intelligent; quite efficient and enterprising. For some years now we've worked with his offic."

"Who? You mean Intelligence?"

"Yes, he built up a financial consulting firm; his was one of the few espionage channels in the Arkonide Imperium that we could do anything with. So now here's Banavol with the Chief and the subject is Cardif. And there's another point, incidentally, where the Chief has changed: he's more persistent than ever before in his efforts to locate his son. The only thing is, I don't know if it's a desirable change or not. Anyway, right now we have other things to worry about."

Neither of them knew, however, the things this man had to worry about that they took to be Perry Rhodan.

* * * *

The man sitting opposite Cardif-Rhodan appeared to be a typical Arkonide. Banavol was about 30 years old by Arkonide reckoning and openly flaunted his arrogance. To him the First Administrator of the Solar Imperium was a member of a lower and more primitive species. He had hardly seated himself before he opened the conversation.

"We both know that between *us* there is no need to

THE MAN WITH TWO FACES

discuss the subject of Thomas Cardif, Terran. Can I speak freely here? What I mean is: not overheard!"

This threw Cardif into a crisis of alarm. Banavol's impudent words were an indication that he had a message of the greatest importance. There was a flash of response in Cardif's eyes but it was the only visible sign of his excitement.

"Can I speak freely here?" Banavol repeated insistently. When his question still went unanswered, the Arkonide appeared to relax unconcernedly. "Very well. It's no concern of mine. I have come here directly from the Crystal World. Fut-gli is waiting for a reply to his greetings, Terran!"

The threatening innuendo failed to elicit a contradiction. Cardif smiled thinly.

The Arkonide continued. "Well, I am doing what I'm getting paid for. But they're not paying me for making long speeches. Rhobal wants 20 cell activators! And with that I've earned my money, Terran. I wouldn't know what else to say."

Something of menace lingered in Benavol's voice and attitude; its threat seemed to lurk within his red Arkonide eyes. Yet he sat there in apparent unconcern.

Cardif-Rhodan's reaction had deceived him, however.

Rhodan's image, seated opposite him, had not twinged or uttered a whimper when the name of the high priest Rhobal was mentioned. He had shown even less reaction when Banavol voiced the Anti's demand: 20 cell activators! 20 antimutants were desirous of acquiring an eternal life like that of the Imperator Gonozal VIII. The only person who could provide them with these egg-sized activators was Rhodan's double, Thomas Cardif.

In their minds it would be easy for him to obtain the

THE MAN WITH TWO FACES

galactic coordinates of the synthetic world Wanderer. The Antis knew thru Cardif that *It* was Rhodan's friend. In the opinion of the Baalol priests it would be a minor task for Cardif to locate Wanderer, request 20 cell activators from *It* and return with the miracle devices.

"Banavol, inform Rhobal that his request is unfeasible," said Cardif.

The Arkonide shrugged. "I'm not authorized to negotiate with you, Terran. If Rhobal's request doesn't suit you, you can complain about it at the Springer base on Pluto. They are waiting there for you before you fly to Wanderer. It's a good thing you reminded me of that or I'd have forgotten to mention it."

Since the beginning of the Solar Imperium no one had ever spoken in this tone before to the First Administrator. But apparently Banavol knew that the man across from him was not Perry Rhodan. The Antis must have entrusted their greatest secret to him.

Thomas Cardif had lived among the antimutants for almost 50 years. There was no Terran who knew the insidious priests better than himself. But for that very reason he knew that Banavol was not a threat, because whenever the Anitis assigned tasks of this nature to anyone, such messengers were no longer free to act of their own volition. So Banavol must be in the same inextricable position as himself—trapped by some extortion of the Baalol priests.

"I'll stay a little longer," said Banavol, "so that my visit will take up an appropriate amount of time. And now, Terran, I'd like to discuss the subject of Thomas Cardif. With your permission, at first I couldn't believe it when Rhobal paid me a visit and related a certain secret to me. But some time later I saw the famous Perry

THE MAN WITH TWO FACES

Rhodan. Cardif, you look beter than he does. There is nothing much left of your father's former greatness. But isn't it strange that the Antis are a thousand times more in awe of a powerless Perry Rhodan than they are of his son? Do you understand me, Terran?"

Thomas Cardif understood exactly what Banavol was saying and why he was saying it. He wanted to make it clear to him again that he was only a marionette for the Antis and that as soon as he ceased to be useful to them they would cast him aside like an empty shell. The permit for an additional 300 commercial bases inside the Sol System was the first step in a bloodless takeover of the Solar Imperium. And he was being used as a catspaw for their plans of conquest!

Some moments passed while each man stared at the other. Thomas Cardif's face still showed no reaction.

"With all due respect, Terran," said Banavol finally, "you have very good self-control. On this point Rhobal did not inform me very well. But now I suppose I can go—or would it be better to stay awhile longer?" The arrogant smile never left his face.

"Why not stay awhile, Arkonide?" answered Cardif. It wasn't said in a tone of friendliness but he returned the smile.

The 2 men facing each other were equal partners because they were both in the same kind of trap. But while Banavol continued to converse and Rhodan's son sought to meet him in repartee a plan was taking form in his mind. Suddenly he was intrigued by the idea of conforming to Rhobal's demands and also he began to be intrigued by this game of matching his strength with that of the Antis. But he still expressed his refusal to

THE MAN WITH TWO FACES

Banavol. He told this gent of the Antis to advise Rhobal that Cafdif was not plaything in their hands.

"It that your last word, Terran?" inquired Banavol as he prepared to leave the office. "You refuse to fly to Wanderer?"

Cardif's answer was almost imperious in its one. "I'm quite certain I've made myself clear to you, Arkonide!"

"As you wish, Terran. It is not my task to transmit your refusal to the priests. The only place you can do that is at the Springer post on Pluto. I have no further responsibility in the matter."

Cardif could believe him. He knew how the Antis worked. Well, he had nothing against a flight to Pluto, at least, and he had no qualms about meeting an Anti in the disguise of a Springer. For the firstime since taking over Rhodan's role he felt in good spirits. He smiled ironically as Banavol left the room. The smile was still there when he made a videophone call to Bell.

"Yes?" he heard him respond. Bell was only thinking of the Thomas Cardif situation. "Was that Arkonide able to say anything important about Cardif, Perry?"

Cardif-Rhodan made a lightning shift of his thoughts. When he replied he was calm and collected. "Banavol didn't have much significant to say, Fatso—aside from maybe 3 clues that could possibly lead somewhere. But that's not why I've called you. I don't want to lose sight of what Mercant had on his mind. Do you follow me? I'm talking about the proposal of the Galactic Traders. I'd like to go along with him and see that approval changed—to the extent that the Springsr will only be allowed to set up 100 new commercial bases a year in the Imperium . . ."

THE MAN WITH TWO FACES

"Perry!" Bell interrupted with enthusiasm. "Are you putting out some of those telepathic tendrils again? You just read my thoughts! That was exactly what I was intending to do but I wanted to have it all laid out first before I showed you the changes."

Cardif maintained his friendly expression altho inwardly boiling over Bell's arbitrary action. Very smoothly he replied: "I can't quite rely on my telepathic ability yet—not that it was ever very much in the first place—but I'm glad we are both agreed on this."

This only served to remind Bell that we was not in agreement at all with allowing Springers into the Sol System in the first place. But he thought he had found a favorable moment for changing Rhodan's mind entirely. "Hey, Perry," he suggested, "don't you think we ought to tell these star gypsies to shove their whole ballawax? All those greedy sky-peddlers can give us is grief in the long run, so I say later with them!"

Now Cardif-Rhodan's tone was noticeably cooler. "I have my own special plans for the Springers." He hoped that this would be enough to dampen Bell's curiosity but it wasn't.

"What plans are you talking about, Perry?"

"I'll tell you more about them later. But don't issue the revised approval of the Springer proposal yet. Before that I want to take another look at their trading post on Pluto." He watched Bell's face carefully on the videoscreen.

But his heavyset listener only laughed. "Now you've really got me curious about your plan, Perry! Galloping galaxies—what's Pluto got to do with those trouble merchants?"

"That you will know soon enough, my friend."

THE MAN WITH TWO FACES

"That 'soon enough' bit is another one of your broken records, Perry," Bell commented pointedly. "But I'm cutting off so I can advise Mercant about the proposal. When are you taking off for Pluto?"

"Probably tomorrow, That's all, Bell."

The videophone shut off. Cardif-Rhodan got up and walked to the window. How often his father had stood here and looked out over the rooftops of Terrania at the landscape beyond, which had all been a desert not too long ago. How often Rhodan had been here alone with his problems, big and small, struggling thru the years for decisions!

It was now much the same for his son, except that his problems were in another category. Everything that he considered or planned was basically on the other side of legality—nothing more than one crime after another. And how had it all come about?

"Rhodan . . ." he heard himself say bitterly, and the hate for his father flamed up anew within him.

In taking over the role of Rhodan he had played the wrong number in this cosmic shell game. His neck was out. For better or worse he was totally dependent upon the Antis. Thru Banavol they had put in an order for 20 cell activators. When Thomas Cardif thought of this he smiled grimly. It wasn't difficult to imagine what the motivations were for such a request: 20 of the most influential Baalol priests were toying with the idea of reaching for relative immortality by means of the activators.

Cardif nodded in secret satisfaction.

His plan was shaping up more and more. It was to become a test of power between his and the Antis and he was convinced now that he would win that contest.

THE MAN WITH TWO FACES

"Alright," he muttered aloud to himself. "So be it!"

In the mist of distance a gigantic shadow swept across the Earth. One of the Solar Fleet's superbattleships was coming in for a landing. The *Wellington* was returning from a mission.

* * * *

Pucky the mousebeaver had a visitor in his own house, which was a comfortable bungalow on the edge of the Goshun salt lake. Rhodan's oldest and most intimate colleagues and friends lived here in this residential colony. Life was grand and peaceful here, far removed from the rush and bustle of Terrania. But in spite of this, Pucky's visitor seemed to be unusually troubled. Even the mousebeaver's mood was not the best at the moment because his incisor tooth remained hidden and the rascally twinkle was absent from his shining mouse eyes.

5 minutes of silence had gone by before Pucky finally chirped a remark. "An icicle is nothing, John, compared to *him*!"

John Marshall, Chief of the Mutant Corps, was the best telepath other than Pucky within his group. He nodded in agreement since the bitter comment was all too appropriate. All he could do in his mind was underline the statement for emphasis. Ever since the Chief had returned from Okul he had continued to build up an invisible wall around himself. It was increasingly noticeable to his old friends that he was no longer the Perry Rhodan they had known but rather the *Administrator* alone—a lonely celebrity, unapproachable and frighteningly impersonal.

Pucky lay on his daybed and John Marshall had stretched himself out in a suspended hammock couch. Be-

THE MAN WITH TWO FACES

side the housebeaver was an assortment of fresh carrots which Pucky had personally grown in his garden. Aware of his obligations as a host, he reached into the mountainous heap and picked out one of the finest specimens. "One for you, John?"

To his surprise the telepath didn't turn down the offer as he usually did. "Yes, hand it over! Vitamins can't hurt at a time like this. Carrots are good for the brain and mine's beat! Pucky—just between the two of us, I have a question: can you still pick up the Chief's thoughts?"

There was an old standing regulation that prohibited the telepaths from using their paranormal faculties in relation to Perry Rhodan or any of his top staff of coworkers. Their thought patterns were forbidden territory and John Marshall had always been among those mutants who had taken care to see that the order was obeyed. On the other hand, Pucky had always been one of the worst offenders in this regard and had not even drawn the line where it came to Rhodan's thoughts. Today, however, even Marshall was ready to violate the rules.

"Yes, John, I can reach his thoughts. But whenever I tune in on his wavelength I get the shudders. What have those medicos done to him? John, have you noticed how little the Chief seems to care about whether or not this lousy Liquitiv curse is wiped out? Even the Swoons, the little cucumber people, feel they've been betrayed and sold out, because the Boss never sees them anymore. I'm telling you, if I knew that the medicos were to blame for Perry's change I'd take that whole cloud-nosed crowd of hippocratic oafs and give them a douse of salts in the lake!"

"Take it easy, little buddy..."

THE MAN WITH TWO FACES

But Pucky wasn't to be deterred now in expressing himself. "So how come you're here to see me if I can't say what I think about our Chief? No matter how often I sneak into his thoughts I can't tap the patterns that used to be there—the ones that were always concerned with Thomas Cardif! Doesn't he ever think of his misguided son anymore?"

"You mean you've changed your opinion about Cardif, Pucky?"

"I had to, John. Now I'm even sorry for all the times I stood up for him.. But tell me now—in these past weeks haven't you also done some snooping around in the Chief's head? Go ahead, John, you can level with me. I wouldn't snitch on you even if we have a few spats now and then. Haven't you noticed something peculiar about him?"

In some surprise, John Marshall straightened up. "What do you mean, Pucky?"

"If I only knew! Since that crazy shock treatment the Chief has turned into somebody else. He can't read thoughts anymore and as far as technical things go, I know more than he does now. He doesn't know how to laugh anymore. But all that's beside the point. There's something in his brain pan that wasn't there before—something strange and kind of blurry. Sometimes when I try to read his mind it's like standing in front of a frosted glass screen and behind that screen I see shadows . . . phantom thought shapes in the background, as tho they were hiding. Then it all clears away—the shadows and the screen along with them. Have you ever noticed that, John?"

The Mutant Corps chief stared long and thoughtfully at the mousebeaver. It was an effort to face the truth.

THE MAN WITH TWO FACES

"Little one, you've just put your finger on something that's been bothering me. Yes, I've seen those shadows! Ye cosmic gods!—do you think those phantoms are the key to what's changed him?"

Even the best telegraphs in the Solar Imperium did not suspect that the *shadows* were actually the thought impulses of Thomas Cardif which had been buried under the hypnotically-implanted knowledge of Rhodan.

After awhile Marshall spoke again. "Pucky, from now on we'll have to keep a sharp watch over the Chief to prevent him from making any disastrous mistakes. It's enough to drive one to despair when you think of all the damage Rhodan's only son has caused."

"Galactic Enemy Number One! I'd have never dreamed I'd say such a thing about Thomas. But in spite of his genius he must be psychopathic."

"Insane with hate for his father; and on top of it a man of 2 different worlds—half Terran, half Arkonide."

Pucky nodded his agreement but added: "In spite of everything I can't understand how a man could walk over dead bodies in order to destroy his own father."

"Don't forget the Antis, little one. Cardif is in their power and once they have somebody in their clutches they never let him go. Cardif has to dance to their tune. He is no longer the master of his own will."

10 ADVENTURES FROM NOW
Kurt Mahr describes
Death's Demand

2/ THE EXTORTIONIST

"Now things are getting *real* cute!" exclaimed Bell in complete exasperation.

He glanced sharply at the intercom which had just brought him a message from Rhodan. Then he got up from his desk and went out. While going thru the outer reception room he snapped: "I'll be in Mercant's office."

When the outer door had closed behind him, someone was heard to say: "Old Chubby's mood gets worse as the Chief gets weirder!"

By this time Bell was already headed below in the antigrav shaft, en route to Solar Marshal Allan D. Mercant. Halfway down the shaft he met Prof. Manoli on his way up.

"Just the man I wanted to see!" shouted the red-haired Solar First Deputy. "Wait a sec, I'm changing floors!"

He moved into the upward force flow, sailed a few meters higher and came out at the next level with the Professor in tow.

"You going to see the Chief?"

Manoli looked at him in astonishment. "Yes, but how did you know that? Rhodan gave me strict orders to keep my visit a secret."

Bell concealed his own surprise. "Do you know why he wants to see you, Prof?"

"He wants a post-treatment checkup."

Bell nodded. "Maybe with enough time I'll get used to Perry's cloak and dagger antics. Did Marshall and Pucky see you, Manoli?"

THE MAN WITH TWO FACES

"A few hours ago, sir. I take it you've been informed, right?"

"And how! What do you make of these *shadows* in Rhodan's brainwaves?"

The Professor shrugged somewhat helplessly. "Unfortunately we are not telepaths. Our equipment can't come near to matching the abilities of a mind reader. So all we have to go on is their own data, which is anything but reliable from a medical standpoint. We need curves, values, charts. We would have to have precise measurements of the intensities . . ."

"So you and your buddies don't have any of that," Bell interrupted. "I'd like to get your private opinion of the Chief, Manoli. Is Perry healthy or sick? Yes or no—no fooling around!"

This was typical of his nature: no fooling around. He always preferred to strike to the bottom line, straight out. He had often taken some awful nosedives this way but just as often he had beat everyone else to the punch.

Being accustomed to think only in medical terms, Manoli tried to squirm out but Bell's merciless glare finally forced him to express a personal view. "The Chief is well, Mr. Bell. It's only that he suffers from a certain depressiveness . . ."

Bell thought he hadn't heard him correctly. "What's he suffering from? You mean he's in the dumps or something? And that you call healthy? Come on now, don't you know by now that Rhodan's mentality isn't geared for depressive thinking? How come you don't buy this bit about the *shadows* that Marshall and Pucky noticed?"

"Because medical science has no knowledge of *shadows* appearing in brainwave patterns! What the 2 telepaths say they've seen is layman nonsense! Mr. Bell,

THE MAN WITH TWO FACES

what do you think would happen if the Chief caught onto the fact that the mutants are poking around in his thoughts . . . ?"

This was the wrong way to go with Bell, who interrupted him abruptly. "What do you think that *I* will do to you, my dear Manoli, if you tell Rhodan anything about it? Do we understand each other?"

"You just made yourself quite clear!" replied Manoli, obviously shocked.

In a friendlier tone, Bell added: "Let me know the results of your examination, please."

"No—! Bell, there's no way I can do that. I'm a doctor. The code of ethics . . ."

"Jam the code of ethics!" Whereat Bell left the bewildered Professor standing there. His former comrade from the long-ago moon-landing project in the 20th century had never spoken to him in this tone before. Until now they had always been the best of friends. When Bell disappeared into the lift shaft, Manoli continued to stare at the spot where he had last seen him.

THE MAN WITH TWO FACES

Could there really be anything to the observations the 2 telepaths had made, he asked himself—but why couldn't they give him a better explanation of these ominous shadows? When he continued on his way to the Chief's office he decided to give him more than the usual checkup.

* * * *

Meanwhile Bell was already in a surface car and had driven to the headquarters of Solar Intelligence. "Is Mercant in?" he asked as he entered the reception lobby of the big building.

"Yessir. Solar Marshal Mercant is in his office.

Shortly thereafter, Bell was seated across from him.

"Well?" asked Mercant unsuspectingly.

"I see you're sitting down, Mercant. These days it's a good idea to be in our seats when either one of us comes in to say anything. The *Ironduke* is being cleared for takeoff."

"I'm aware of that, Mr. Bell."

"OK, so nothing special about that, right?" retorted Bell with a slight note of sarcasm. "But why the Chief has cleared the *Ironduke* for just a little toad-hop to Pluto . . . well, is that something else again, Mercant?"

Mercant's eyes narrowed cautiously. "You mean—the *Ironduke* is only going to Pluto?"

"So you don't have any idea about the second step, do you, Solar Marshal? I learned about it by pure accident. It often happens in Terrania that even the top-drawer secrets can't be buried. Perry called the positronic brain on Venus and asked for the galactic coordinates of *Wanderer!*"

THE MAN WITH TWO FACES

Mercant's words were like an explosion. "The Chief wants to go *there*—?!"

"Yes, Mercant. A little more of this and I'm going up in smoke, with Perry's help. He's never lied to me before. But a short while ago he handed me a whopper! What do you say to that, my friend?"

"Nothing, before I know what the Chief is planning. I suspect he has something big on his mind. Perhaps I can guess his purpose: he may be hoping to regain our shaken confidence in him by pulling off some very surprising action."

"You still believe in Santa Claus!" cried Bell. "But I wonder if it could be possible..."

"What?" asked Mercant.

"Nothing!" Bell waved it off. He had hoped to meet with understanding here in the office of the Solar Marshal, to find a reasoning partner who might also be convinced as he was that something was very wrong with Perry Rhodan. And what was the result? Mercant believed the Chief wanted to pull a big surprise on everybody so that he could regain their confidence in him. "Glord!" he groaned aloud.

Mr. Bell, I almost have to assume that you're biased toward an idea that isn't at all related to the facts," said Mercant in a tone of slightly-irritated reproach.

Bell shook his head moodily. "Assume what you want, Mercant, I'll not yield on one point, and that's Perry's condition—he's really sick, mentally or psychologically. On the way to see you I ran into Prof. Manoli. He'd been called by the Chief to give him another checkup. But that's a secondary matter. I know the Chief like nobody else and when I say he's changed you'd better believe it!

THE MAN WITH TWO FACES

"Sometimes he seems to be his old self when he starts to make a lightning decision. Then he seems closer to me and I know what's going on. But as soon as he pulls back into his shell and starts making decisions under a lid, all by himself—then I'm looking at a stranger.

"Now Rhodan has lied to me! He gave me the old 84* when he put on that he simply had to go to Pluto—telling me it was of critical importance for him to inspect the Springer layout there. Mercant, since when has he bothered about such minor details? What's Solar Intelligence for? And if he only wants to hop to Pluto, why take the *Ironduke*? Why the request to the Venus Brain for the galactic coordinates of Wanderer? What's our business on Wanderer at this time?"

"But Mr. Bell, are you saying that I should put the Chief under surveillance or somehing?" At least Mercant's protest revealed that Bell's words had made an impression on him.

"Who's talking about surveillance? He's supposed to be healthy! But I'm more convinced than ever that if he's sick it isn't from any so-called depressive condition, which Manoli was trying to sell me. No—the Chief is hiding another kind of sickness..."

"Thomas Cardif?"

"That's my bet. When that kid got the upper hand on his father there on Okul, something in Perry must have snapped. Forget low spirits and depression! Since Okul, something's been missing from him completely: the human touch, maybe, a spirit of animation, *zombop!* Mercant, what I'm trying to say can't quite be described!"

* Doubletalk

THE MAN WITH TWO FACES

"Are you saying that he never speaks of his experiences with his son on Okul?" Mercant appeared to be more convinced now that Bell's concern for Rhodan might be well-founded.

The video intercom rattled out an announcement: "Attention, urgent message: takeoff schedule for the *Ironduke* has been advanced to hours 18:35, standard time. I repeat: takeoff schedule for the *Ironduke* ..."

Bell cut the connection swiftly. The speaker's metallic clamor had suddenly grated on his nerves. "Are you flying with him, Mercant?"

"I've received no orders to do so."

"Nor I. But I'll be on board. In fact John Marshall is there already with some of his veteran mutants."

Mercant let out a low whistle. "Mr. Bell, you're sure sticking your neck out! I don't know what the Chief's reaction will be when he finds out you and the mutants are on board."

Bell laughed bitterly. "And think what a surprise it'll be when he also finds *you* there, Mercant!"

The latter stared at him thru a moment of frozen silence but finally took a long deep breath. "You know, Mr. Bell, ever since you began to suspect that Rhodan isn't himself, you've developed some faculties I would never have expected of you. Alright, I'll join you on board."

Bell left his office without having mentioned how very exposed he considered his own neck to be.

* * * *

The vast steel sphere of the *Ironduke* dropped down toward Pluto. At 20,000 meters the ship's searchlights

THE MAN WITH TWO FACES

flared to life and illuminated the desolate, hostile surface of the Sol System's next-to-outermost planet.

Out of quadrant Green, 30 degrees, came the instrument approach beam of stellar defense fortress Pluto-6. The guide beam touched the ship, ready to bring it in on computer course. The nearer the *Ironduke* came to the surface, the mightier loomed the gun installations of the base in the glare of the lights.

Here were the heaviest-calibre thermo-cannons and on either side of them the disintegrator and impulse batteries became visible. A few km farther south were the powerful tracking and sensor stations which were capable of detecting any transitional spacewarp in the outer void and tracking approaching vessels over tremendous distances. The main base's towering antennas were under a super-powerful defense screen that could hold up against salvos from half a dozen superbattleships.

Even during the landing maneuvers of the *Ironduke* the great screen was not shut off. This was by strict orders from Cardif-Rhodan himself. He had also requested alternate beam course to the small spaceport which the Galactic Traders had established by use of their own equipment and materials. On the eastern edge of the port under the sheltering cliffs of an ice-covered mountain chain was the trading settlement of the united Springer clans. This was Cardif-Rhodan's goal.

What his objective was in this visit to the Springers was a mystery to everyone on the ship but this wasn't the first action the Chief had started in which only he knew the purpose. Nevertheless there was such a high level of tension in the Control Central that it fairly crackled.

THE MAN WITH TWO FACES

Was it because of the big surprise only a few minutes before when Reginald Bell walked in unannounced with Allan D. Mercant and John Marshall? Even Jefe Claudrin the Epsalian-born Terran—a stocky colossus with dark leathery skin—was heard to gasp harshly when he saw the 3 men enter and simultaneously he swore he was going to haul a certain airlock officer over the coals for not having reported these people on board.

Other than a momentary gleam in his eyes, Cardif-Rhodan had not revealed any sign of surprise. "Oh—!" was all that came from his lips and then he merely nodded to Bell.

While Mercant and Marshall remained in the background, Bell came forward without hesitation. "I had enough of this during those last hours on Okul, Jerry," he said to the man he still thought to be his friend. "This visit you're making—I mean, I don't trust these sky gypsies any more than I do the Antis!"

"So?" Cardif-Rhodan answered. "The nextime, Fatso, I exepct to be informed about your security measures—do you understand?"

Bell only shrugged and the incident was ended. But no one suspected the inner turmoil he had caused in Cardif, not even John Marshall, who now tuned into the Chief's thoughts for the third time. Rhodan's double deliberately maintained a fragmentary train of thought. He guessed that Marshall was giving him a mental surveillance, which he compensated for as calmly as possible. Cardif-Rhodan only thought on his father's wavelengths and completely concealed his own impulses.

In his cogitations the proposal of the Galactic Traders played the heaviest role, with here and there tatters and fragments of memories out of the past. The pseudo-

THE MAN WITH TWO FACES

Rhodan thought of former treacherous maneuvers of the Springers and he began to calculate how great the danger might be if the Traders established another 100 commercial bases inside the Sol System. He allowed his thoughts to circulate to this extent but he was careful not to think of what lay beyond that. Only a few times he permitted a surge of anticipation and hopeful triumph, picturing an end result where the Galactic Traders would turn out to be the swindlers who were betrayed.

Meanwhile under Jefe Claudrin's guidance the *Ironduke* had made a safe landing at the Springers' spaceport. The mighty telescopic struts of the gigantic sphere had made a few feathery contacts before the ship settled firmly on the frozen soil of Pluto, at a distance of more than 20 km from Pluto-6 and its bristling defenses.

The tense atmosphere caused by the appearance of Bell, Mercant and Marshall now reached a new high. The man whom everybody took to be Rhodan laughed at Bell in a strangely crafty tone.

"Just so you won't try to play nursemaid nextime I'm taking the liberty of playing this one solo. And when I say alone, I mean just that! I'm visiting the Springer post *without* an escort. Let me have a spacesuit, please . . ."

The Epsalian commander's mighty hands clenched the arms of his special flight seat. He simply could not comprehend what he had just heard. But he was not the only one who couldn't understand Rhodan's actions.

"Sir—" Allan D. Mercant started to protest but was forced to silence by a swift signal from Cardif-Rhodan.

Against all expectations, Bell said nothing.

By now Rhodan was inside the heavy spacesuit. With an exemplary calmness he inspected his weapons. Since

THE MAN WITH TWO FACES

the first encounter with the Antis, everyone's armament included an old-fashioned .44 revolver with non-metallic bullets. The special plastic bullet heads had an astonishing penetrating power. At present these bullets were the only means of breaking thru the priests' bodily defense screens, which they rendered super powerful by mental forces.

Cardif-Rhodan merely gave the old-fashioned weapon a passing glance. He was more interested in his energy weapons and he checked out their charge readings.

"All set," he announced. "Bell, I think I'll be back in about an hour. Emergency communications by minicom. Thank you," he said when he noted that Bell was about to accompany him, "I'd also like to go alone to the airlock. Somehow I'll have to show you my appreciation for all your precautions, my friend."

It could have been a jest—but also sarcasm.

The bulkhead hatch slammed shut behind Cardif-Rhodan. Bell looked questioningly at Mercant. He winked at him secretly and then left the control room. Shortly afterwards he was followed by Mercant and Marshall. Purposefully they sought out Bell's cabin.

"Well?" he asked them as they came in. His question was really directed at Marshall.

The telepath shrugged helplessly. "The Chief has some wild plan in his mind—about the Springers and the 300 additional stations—but unfortunately he didn't do me the favor of thinking it out. I only know that at this particular Springer post he's looking for something specific..."

"What's that?" Bell interrupted.

"That's just what I don't know. He kept it out of his

THE MAN WITH TWO FACES

mind somehow. As for our unexpected arrival, he wasn't a bit disturbed about it..."

"What?" Bell jumped up and stared at Marshall. "John, don't give me any fairytales! Look—we came here completely unauthorized, strictly AWOL! You mean to say he didn't show a trace of steam? What the devil! Any other time he'd be ready to chew me out for going against his orders like that. Has he been mentally turned inside out or something?"

"There's nothing more I can say," replied Marshall.

"Then I'm stumped for *what* I should think!" grumbled Bell, and he sat down again. He put the subject aside but asked Marshall another question. "Do you have contact with the other telepaths on board?"

"They are waiting for your instructions, Mr. Bell."

"OK, so let's wait for another half hour. At the moment, all the *Ironduke's* polar gun turret is doing is keeping close tabs on the Springer movements out there. I have to presume that those sky-hoppers won't try anything with the Chief—not here. Anyway, Perry did a beautiful job of pulling the rug out from under us with this solo caper of his. And I'm glad of it! It's more typical of him. There's some hope yet that he may come around to his old self again. Well, Mercant, what do you say?"

"Nothing," was the reply. "I'll wait and see..."

* * * *

Catepan, Springer chief of the Pluto trading base, had sent his biggest groundcar out to the *Ironduke*. The vehicle was waiting for the First Administrator at the foot of C-ramp, which had extended outward from the spherical ship.

THE MAN WITH TWO FACES

Fearless, cold-blooded, calm, Cardif-Rhodan came down the ramp. He was quite familiar with the hostile environment of Pluto. As a lieutenant in the Solar Fleet, Cardif had been transferred here for disciplinary reasons and had put in some service time, until all of a sudden the mighty alien fleet of the Druufs challenged the Sol System's defenses. At that time the fate of the Earth appeared to be sealed but then Arkon's robot fleets came to the rescue along with the Galactic Traders and their fighting long-ships.

At that time—he thought only fleetingly of it but not about his desertion. He switched his thoughts quickly. As he returned to Rhodan's wavelengths a grin came to his face that would have been alien to Rhodan himself. It was an expression of cynical satisfaction. The mutants, whom he had first considered to be his greatest danger, foundered against the hypno-induced knowledge of the genuine Rhodan, a surface screen which served to conceal Thomas Cardif. And since they continued to sense Rhodan's mental patterns they did not suspect that this very corroboration was their obstacle.

The young Springer's face was illuminated by the spotlight of the car as he greeted the First Administrator of the Solar Imperium. In good Interkosmo he invited him to take a seat inside the vehicle. Cardif-Rhodan curtly acknowledged the greeting and then sank back into the car's upholstered seat.

The machine sped like a shot across the smooth pavement of the landingfield. Under indirect lighting the vast outlines of the Springer installations began to become more discernible. A hall-sized airlock received the car. The driver opened the door for him and greeted him

THE MAN WITH TWO FACES

again as he got out. The young chauffeur advised him that he could open his plastic space helmet.

The man in the uniform of the highest official on Earth thanked him for his courtesy and then turned toward the Galactic Trader who was hurrying toward him: Catepan, chief patriarch of the Springer post on Pluto.

Later in Catepan's office the patriarch offered a seat to the Administrator. Only here in the private suite of the Springer did Cardif-Rhodan decide to remove his helmet, which he did with a special purpose. Thereby he broke off his radio connection with the *Ironduke*.

"Catepan," he said immediately, "you are probably familiar with the proposal of the Galactic Traders who want to establish new commercial centers within the sphere of interest of the Solar Imperium. I shall approve that proposal if I don't find any reasons here for rejecting it."

The old Trader regarded him in amazement. "But—Administrator, are you saying that *this* is why you have come here personally?"

"That's right." Altho Cardif-Rhodan spoke casually he concealed his real satisfaction. Catepan had plainly indicated that he took him for Administrator Rhodan. Cardif needed to know no more. When he got up again and Catepan rose up also as if to accompany him, he waved him off. "Thank you, Catepan, I'll go alone. Don't worry, I won't go astray in your rooms and offices. You may expect me back here in half an hour."

When he went out he left an oldtime veteran Springer standing there in utter confusion. Catepan couldn't get it into his head that the mightiest man in the Solar Im-

THE MAN WITH TWO FACES

perium was concerning himself with such an inconsequential item as a mere trading post; and even less could he understand why Perry Rhodan himself had come personally and alone. But the most inexplicable part of it all was what the Pluto trading post itself had to do with the major proposal of the combined Springer clans.

Meanwhile Cardif-Rhodan had left the section designated for offices and living quarters and had traversed a bright passage which brought him into the first of the storage areas. His glances to right and left were only cursory because he was hardly concerned with the trade goods that were stacked here. The chief point of interest now was the Springer who stood in front of a door at the end of the warehouse. He appeared to be waiting for him—yet as Cardif approached the man, the latter turned his back to him and disappeared into the passage behind him.

Cardif recalled what the Arkonide Banavol had told him. It was only here in this Springer base that he would be able to make his protest against the Antis' demand for 20 cell activators from Wanderer. Was this man he had just seen the agent of the priests of Baalol? Cardif had to know. Before going thru the doorway he turned to look back. The storage hall he had traversed was more than 50 meters wide and 100 meters long. He wanted to make sure no one had followed him.

Having confirmed this he nodded with satisfaction and still paused there to savor a growing realization. Even here, he thought, in this extra-territorial location, the wish of the First Administrator was law! A sense of power swept over Cardif like an overwhelming euphoria. The indescribable awareness of only having to give an

THE MAN WITH TWO FACES

order to fulfill all of his wishes was becoming an obsession that was hard to control. He did not know in this moment that his eyes gleamed with the light of megalomania. He only knew what pleasure it gave him to yield to this delicious state of power consciousness.

Then like a destroying bolt of lightning came the memory of an ultimatum—the demand of Rhobol, high priest of Baalol: 20 cell activators, automatically adjustable to individual wave patterns! The ecstacy of a moment before imploded suddenly into naked reality: disguised as his father, he was inescapably Thomas Cardif—*a puppet!*

He closed his eyes and took a deep breath.

Thus the one moment was gone in which fate offered Thomas Cardif another chance to turn his life into brighter paths. He put it out of his mind. He was ready now for the test of power between him and the antimutants. Here in this trading settlement of the Galactic Traders on Pluto he would launch his plan which would eventually destroy the servants of Baalol.

Thomas Cardif turned and went into the connecting passageway. It led away from the storeroom at a right angle. The first part of the next section had been constructed as a heavy-walled blast shelter in case of catastrophe and was equipped with double airlocks. After the last lock door closed behind him he found himself in a new office section. As he soon discovered, this part was built along the left side of the building compound and faced the Traders' spaceport.

He walked calmly along the hallway which was provided with soundproofed floor covering. Finally he came to a door which was standing open, permitting a view

THE MAN WITH TWO FACES

of the room inside. A man turned from the window in the office and stared straight at him. With a nod of his head he signaled Cardif to enter.

Cardif-Rhodan walked in and gave the door a slight shove so that it closed behind him. The other man looked like a Springer with the typical beard and "star gypsy" clothing.

The stranger bowed and spoke to him in good Interkosmo: "In the name of Fut-gli I am authorized to give greetings to the First Administrator of the Syrola Daquarta—the Solar Imperium."

"Thank you," Cardif replied in a clipped tone. He sounded self-controlled and his gaze was highly indifferent. "May I sit down?" Without waiting for permission he took a seat.

Looking beyond the man, he could see the inhospitable surface of Pluto outside. Part of the Traders' spaceport was visible from here and a most unmistakable object across the field was the mighty sphere of the *Ironduke*, clearly discernible in the glare of its own lights. Cardif looked bored as he turned his gaze back to the Baalol agent—for such the stranger was. Mention of the name of Fut-gli had been identification enough.

"Well?" Cardif demanded caustically.

The Baalol agent remained silent. With arms folded across his chest and leaning back against the window sill, he stared back at the man whom others claimed was Perry Rhodan. Cardif felt a surge of anger. The arrogant attitude of this representative of the priest cult was beginning to get to him.

"I cannot and I will not furnish you your 20 little miracles!" he said abruptly.

THE MAN WITH TWO FACES

"But that you *will* do," replied the other. His face remained inscrutable. "You're going to have to, Cardif, or the days of your power are numbered, not to mention your life!" Then he turned his back on him and looked out toward the looming spaceship from Terra. "What a magnificent dungeon cell for you! The *Ironduke* will surely take you back to Terrania for your final judgment."

"Your mouth is bigger than your brain," sneered Cardif. "You talk far too much. What do you expect to accomplish with threats? What's it going to buy you?"

"Nothing," answered the other as he turned back to face him again, "other than 20 cell activators."

"Extortion?"

"The servants of Baalol are above such a filthy accusation!" retorted the agent.

"You know, for about 60 years now the Springers have also tried to get me to dance on a string but they have never succeeded. Who in the devil are you?"

"I am A-thol, personal representative of the high priest, Rhobal. Any other questions, Cardif?"

"Rhobal's request is not feasible," Cardif answered sharply.

"You have no choice in the matter. On Lepso you swore eternal allegiance and gratitude to the cult of Baalol. Today, Baalol takes you at your word; otherwise in a few days the whole galaxy will have the head of its Public Enemy #1 on a silver platter. One word from us, skillfully planted in the right places, would be enough to rip the mask from your face. Make your choice here, Cardif. Before you leave this room you will have to make your decision."

THE MAN WITH TWO FACES

Cardif was still master of the situation as he asked in frigid tones: "What does the high priest offer in case I deliver?"

For the firstime the Anti's features revealed his thoughts. He grinned derisively. "Great Baalol will then shield you with his mighty hand forever!"

"Oh, he will, will he?" Cardif chanced to look past the antimutant. He looked outside into the twilight zone and discovered something that instantly upset a part of his plan.

Without visible reaction, he adjusted himself to a new situation. He managed not to draw attention to what he had observed.

* * * *

It had become quiet in Bell's cabin. Except for a casual glance, Allan D. Mercant had not been involved in the conversation between Bell and Marshall. Now the 3 men were waiting for a call from Rhodan over the minicom. They had noted with agitation that he had cut off his helmet radio shortly after being greeted by the Springer patriarch Catepan.

After that had come the silence and waiting.

But instead of hearing from Rhodan they received a sudden call from the mutant tele-tracer, Felmer Lloyd. His face appeared on the screen of the intercom.

"Sir, I've picked up the brainwave patterns of an *Anti!*"

That last word was all that was needed.

"Robot detail 1, emergency standby for action" roared Bell. His stocky frame moved quickly to the other mike but now he quickly re-channeled Lloyd's line so that

THE MAN WITH TWO FACES

what the mutant was saying could be heard by everyone on board.

"Anti wave patterns!" Lloyd continued, his voice now coming over all speakers. "At the Springer base! Pattern indications are hate, derision, thoughts of assassination. I'm sorry I didn't get it all. The Anti must have put a mental block into his screen. Attention! Anti brainwave pattern ..."

"OK, thanks!" Bell interrupted. "Put all telepaths to work, Lloyd ... Jefe Claudrin, did you hear all that?"

There was something like a confirmation but it was such a thunderous roar that it overdrove the speakers. Yes, the Epsalian commander of the *Ironduke* had heard.

"Alright, Claudrin, but if these planet swindlers manage to get so much as a lifeboat into space ..."

Now it was Bell's turn to be interrupted.

"So it'll be my neck—yes*sir!*"

Bell was halfway out the cabin when he caught Mercant's grin. In spite of the seriousness of the situation he couldn't help chuckling, himself, over Claudrin's dry repartée.

The 3 men ran for the nearest antigrav shaft while Bell gave instructions over his minicom transceiver. "Robot detail 1! Wait until we get to the airlock! This is a combat alert!"

This time the normally swift shaft seemed to carry them all too slowly toward their goal. En route, Bell contacted Fellmer Lloyd again. There were no further developments. The antimutant in the Springer station was apparently still under his mentally-fortified personal screen. There was no further trace of his thought impulses.

There was one more stop before reaching the outer

THE MAN WITH TWO FACES

airlock. Bell, Mercant and Marshall had to put on their spacesuits. Altho time was of the essence they refused to overlook anything now.

"Weapon check!" Bell ordered, having been the first into his suit.

Mercant and Marshall reported all-clear in the weapons department so they all hastened to the outer lock. Shoulder to shoulder they ran down the ramp. At the bottom was the hovercraft with a crew of 20 combat robots and one robot pilot. The robots were the equivalent of 100 well-trained men of the Solar Fleet when it came to battle action.

The personnel carrier rose from the ground on its antigravs. Its sudden acceleration was almost uncanny. Bell sat beside the big mechanical pilot. He had pulled the panel mike to him but did not make use of it for the moment. He could see their rushing approach toward the Trader base as they glided swiftly along at a 10-meter altitude. He glanced at an instrument on the flight console which measured the distance from the Springer's energy defense screen.

Still 2 kilometers ...

Bell held his silence.

One kilometer!

Now came his challenge: "Springer Catepan, this is Reginald Bell, Rhodan's second-in-command! Open your screen immediately! At once or the *Ironduke* will open fire!"

3 seconds later the instrument needle fell to zero. The energy screen surrounding the Springer base had ceased to exist for the moment.

The hovercraft with its robot and human cargo came down close to the entrance lock of the station. The com-

THE MAN WITH TWO FACES

bat robots swarmed out, perfectly programmed to deploy themselves strategically. Three of them rose on their antigravs to a height of 50 meters where they could cover almost the entire complex of storage warehouses and buildings. The others raced with the men toward the airlock. It opened without any challenge from Bell. When they entered it closed automatically behind them and the inner door also opened. In the hall ahead they could see the Springer patriarch hurrying toward them, showing obvious signs of alarm. He was not wearing a spacesuit. It meant that Bell and his 2 companions could open their helmets, which they did.

"Where is the Administrator!" roared Bell as the Springer chief came up to him.

Catepan's alarm changed to astonishment. "Perry Rhodan? He's back in one of the offices but ..."

"Which offices," Bell interrupted. "Where?"

Completely bewildered, Catepan pointed toward the end of the long warehouse.

"Then behind that to the left?" asked Bell cautiously.

The patriarch simply nodded.

Bell sprinted away. His heavy suit did not seem o retard him. But he had hardly advised the robots of his destination before 17 of them raced past him, arriving at the farther door before he had covered half the distance.

In spirte of his concern for Rhodan, the rugged First Deputy did not forget to inform the men on the *Ironduke*. He called thru to them, using the spacesuit's transceiver. "Claudrin, we're inside the base on our way to the Chief. Robots already gone on ahead. Over and out!"

John Marshall kept pace beside him with Mercant about 10 meters in the rear. They reached the door be-

THE MAN WITH TWO FACES

yond which the 17 robots had already disappeared. They had hardly entered the passageway when Bell suddenly grasped Marshall's arm impulsively and stopped him. "Marshall, what was that?" he yelled. "Was it a shot?"

John Marshall could only nod his confirmation.

* * * *

The Anti had no idea of what was racing toward the base from the *Ironduke* at very low altitude but Cardif-Rhodan had been able to observe its approach.

For a long moment Cardif was gripped by a fear that bordered on panic. He remembered that Bell, Mercant and Marshall had come along on the flight without being authorized or asked to do so. And now he realized that with these men there was probably a group of mutants also on board the *Ironduke*.

Bell and his precautions!

His main cause for alarm was his apprehension that the telepaths might have been able to identify the basic brainwave patterns of the true Thomas Cardif. But then the absolute certainty that his own patterns were blocked from emerging to the surface served to calm him down somewhat. Nevertheless he had to make the most strenuous effort to hold his thoughts in the channels of his father.

That which he planned he dared not even touch with a conscious thought.

This was for him a moment of gravest danger. He had never been so close to being unmasked before. In order to eliminate any possible suspicion on the part of the telepaths he forced himself to build up a mental web of lies in complete detail while weaving it into his father's transferred thought-patterns. In his thoughts he

THE MAN WITH TWO FACES

gave form to the realization that he had just discovered the man across from him to be an Anti!

Thomas Cardif did not realize that in so doing he accomplished something unique enough to be worthy of a better deed.

He proceeded to speak to the Anti; he pointed out the risk that he, the Anti, was taking to show up here in the heart of the Solar Imperium. Nothing more was said about the cell activators nor was Rhodan's name mentioned. The Anti overlooked the fact that Thomas Cardif was suddenly leading the discussion and he also failed to notice that he was keeping it in neutral channels.

But what he knew least of all was that a combat group from the linear-drive ship *Ironduke* had already come into the station. Nevertheless he began to note something sinister in Cardif's attitude. As the latter began to approach him slowly, he was instinctively alerted. "Don't get too close to me, Cardif!" he warned. "I turned on my screen shortly after you came in. Stay where you are—not another step!"

It was then that the first ponderous, metallic steps of the fighter robots rang out in the corridor.

"What's that?" It was the Anti's last question because he made the mistake of going past Cardif to have a look out the door.

A-thol did not see what his visitor quickly whipped out of a pocket of his spacesuit. But as the indirect lighting was reflected from the barrel of an ancient-looking Terran weapon it was already too late to do anything. The non-magnetic plastic bullet crashed thru his superpowerful defense screen and struck home where Thomas Cardif intended it to.

The man in the mask of Perry Rhodan overlooked

THE MAN WITH TWO FACES

nothing now. He changed his grip on the .44 revolver, grasping it by the barrel, and struck the butt-end against the right side of his chin. It tore the skin and drew blood.

Cardif's next move was a swift dash to the desk. Among the papers was a heavy paperweight. Picking it up, he passed it over his bloodied chin, then let it fall to the floor. But in the midst of all this to think unwaveringly of the Antis yet not imagine the cavern location on Okul was an incredible effort of highest mental concentration.

Behind him the door flew open.

2 robots rushed into the room. Thru their ocular systems they registered the presence of the body lying directly in front of the Administrator. Then Cardif was surrounded by a swarm of ponderous combat machines that were followed shortly by Bell and Marshall and finally by Allan D. Mercant.

"Perry!" Bell blurted out as he saw the dead man. "You shot him?" There was a note of puzzled alarm in his voice.

"Any objections, Bell?" Cadrif-Rhodan's voice was harsh and imperious. "Was I supposed to let an Anti get the best of me?" As tho not intended, he let Bell see the wounded side of his chin.

Bell still stood there over the dead Anti. Noticing the paperweight on the floor, he stooped down and picked it up. When he was about to place it on the desk he saw the blood on it. Strange—he thought to himself. But why he thought so he wasn't sure. Was it because in this paricular situation Perry Rhodan had never appeared to be so alien?

Perry had defended himself. Clearly in *self*-defense, of course—but even then, would Perry Rhodan neces-

THE MAN WITH TWO FACES

sarily kill? Couldn't he have shot to wound him instead? Wasn't it Perry Rhodan who had always demanded that human lives were to be spared where possible, under any circumstances?

"You seem to be unhappy about something, Bell," commented Cardif-Rhodan warily. "I demand to know what's on your mind.'

To Bell the question was like a whiplash. He stepped over the body and stood by the desk. Glancing swfitly at Mercant and Marshall he noted that they were also unsettled over what had happened here. Then he looked sharply into his friend's gray eyes which had suddenly become so cold. "Perry, how did you know that this man was an Anti?" he asked.

Cardif-Rhodan smiled thinly. "You have forgotten the visit I had with a certain Arkonide named Banavol. You've given too little thought to why I wanted to visit the Springer station specifically on Pluto. Why? To inspect their base?" He laughed sharply, which brought a look of new surprise from Allan D. Mercant. "I have a few more important things to do, my friend, than to make personal inspections. However, in this case I had to find out for myself if Banavol's suspicion was correct. This dead man verifies his report that an Anti had infiltrated here. Or do you suppose that nowadays the Galactic Traders are also able to mentally strengthen their individual defense screens?"

Bell impatiently waved his argument aside. "But when I came in, Perry, you talked as if you killed him deliberately!"

The other shrugged without the blink of an eyelash.

"Oh, did I? Then either I didn't phrase my words correctly or you misunderstood me."

3/ WHEN "IT" LAUGHED

When they came back to the *Ironduke* an important message from Earth was waiting for them. In Pagny-sur-Moselle, where the European plant for Allitiv production had been set up, the workers and technicians had gone on strike. They were demanding a 20% pay increase. If the strike weren't settled by afternoon of the following day, doctors in Europe would be threatened with a depletion of their Allitiv supplies. What effect this would have on millions of addicted people could not yet be estimated.

Cardif-Rhodan read the emergency dispatch in the Control Central and then handed it over to Bell. "Take care of this," he said curtly.

Bell stared at him perplexedly. It was hardly believable, he thought. Could it be that Perry Rhodan no longer cared whether the narcotic victims in Eurpoe got well or not?

Altho boiling with resentment, he controlled himself. "Alright, Perry—I'll take care of it," he said. And with that he headed for the Communications Room.

On his way there he met Brazo Alkher, the officer of the fire control center. "Well, Alkher, where are you headed?" Bell asked.

"To see the Chief. He called me on his minicom. I don't know yet what he wants, sir."

"Oh? The Chief called you? Well—alright, thank you, Alkher." Bell seemed to speak absentmindedly, was the impression the weapons officer got from Rhodan's First Deputy.

THE MAN WITH TWO FACES

When Bell entered the *Ironduke's* Communications Center he neither greeted nor saluted anyone as was his usual custom. He looked at no one but merely came over next to the hypercom operator and stared at the console panels.

The shavetail lieutenant at that position took one look at him and knew that trouble was brewing. He didn't dare open his mouth.

Bell was trying to solve the mystery of *when* Perry had signaled the fire control officer to come to the Control Central. Because from the moment they had left the dead Anti in the Springer base, he and Rhodan had been together. Was it that Perry had given the weapons officer a call while he was on his way to the Springer station? Those physicians, he thought grimly—what had they done to Perry? Could it be, however, that the Chief's new and incomprehensible characteristics were *not* due to the Thmasson shock therapy?

Finally he snapped out of his broodings and seemed to realize where he was. "Oh—ah—yes! Send the following dispatch to the hypercom station in Europe: Concerning strike in Allitiv plant, Pagny-sur-Moselle. The Administration takes recouse to Section 43, paragraph 2 and declares a state of emergency for the Allitiv plant at your location. Emergency status to take effect at zero hours. All striking personnel to be advised that any further refusal to work will be punishable by imprisonment. Signed: Reginald Bell."

"Is this to be coded, sir?" asked the young operator.

"Clear text!" growled Bell. "I'll teach those people in Pagny-sur-Moselle not to capitalize on a desperate situation like this. Wait, friend! Let's change that last sentence. Finish it up like this: All striking personnel to be

THE MAN WITH TWO FACES

advised that any further refusal to work will be punishable by *deportation*. The Administration refers to Section 1, paragraph 1 of the emeregncy provisions. Signed: Reginald Bell . . . I think that's more to the point. Damnation! I'll go along with any legitimate strike but this one is piracy!"

Without another word he stamped out of the Com Room. Unsuspectingly, he returned to the Control Central.

Jefe Claudrin was standng in the middle of the room like a brass statue. His eyes fairly burned a hole in the Chief as he stared at him. Perry Rhodan turned his back on Bell as he came in.

"That is the way it will be, Claudrin! You are to remain with the *Ironduke* on Pluto. Ready a space-jet for takeoff! Nolinov, Alkher! You know what you have to do!"

The 2 young lieutenants stood before Rhodan and saluted sharply. "Yessir!" they snapped in unison, and turned to leave.

But Bell blocked their way. "Where to?" he asked.

The other officers present in the Control Central had been looking back and forth from the Chief to the commander but now they stared only at Perry Rhodan, who was standing about 20 feet from Bell and facing him.

"Bell, may I ask that you do not delay the lieutentenants?" he ordered more than asked.

The red-headed First Deputy glared at Rhodan with a hard gleam in his eyes. He took another look at the 2 lieutenants and then answered with equal sharpness in his voice. "I'd like to know why a space-jet's taking off! To my knowledge, all jets are in standby readiness—standard procedure."

THE MAN WITH TWO FACES

Jefe Claudrin stepped in front of the Chief and saved him the trouble of answering—but he had a special purpose: to tell Bell what had happened in his absence. "The Chief wants to fly alone to Wanderer—with these 2 men. He can't use the *Ironduke*."

It made no sense to Bell. There was no ship in this section of the galaxy that was faster and safer than the *Ironduke*. Couldn't Perry see that right now everything was going haywire with him—that he was more vulnerable to mishaps than ever before? What did he want to do—*force* a catastrophe on himself? For weeks now he'd been practically insulting to one and all. It was enough to drive a man up the bulkheads, he thought dejectedly.

Then he astonished everyone by just saying "OK" and stepping aside so that the 2 officers could pass. He had seen a well-known flash in Rhodan's eyes which was typical of the Chief. It meant that no power in the world could deter him now from flying in the space-jet to Wanderer.

Besides, Bell was in no mood for fighting windmills. He didn't know when he had ever felt as dispirited as he had in the past few hours.

* * * *

Space-jet I-109 had disappeared into the depths of the outer void. The *Ironduke's* hypersensor system had tracked the small craft's transition entry.

"Flight on course!" was Jefe Claudrin's brief announcement.

And why shouldn't it be, he thought, with the two-man team the Chief had selected?

Stana Nolinov, commander of the *Ironduke's* robot forces, was just like weapons officer Brazo Alkher—un-

THE MAN WITH TWO FACES

pretentious but a hard-bitten young veteran and ready for anything. However, the daring gallantry of these two was not their chief characteristic. In emergency situations when there was no time to think, they were both capable of acting instinctively and doing the right thing at the right time.

They hadn't exactly learned these things during their training period in the Solar Space Academy but shrewd psychologists had recognized the invaluable talents that were slumbering in the two of them and understanding instructors had been able to bring out these hidden capabilities, developing their reactive faculties to the point of automation.

Brazo Alkher was at the flight controls of the I-109. The position coordinates of Wanderer had been dumped into the smaller ship's nav-computer from the *Ironduke's* main positronicon banks. Some time before, the vast brain on Venus had spent a number of hours working them out.

Alkher and Nolinov were alone in the control room. The Chief had withdrawn to his cabin. Altho the disc-shaped flier was only 35 meters in diameter and was a mere seed pod in comparison to any of the heavier class spherical ships, it offered everything that might be expected of a proper space vehicle. Equipped with the most modern hyperspace propulsion and the finest automatic pilot system, it was even superior to many larger ships of other galactic races, and where its armaments were concerned, no space-jet was to be underestimated. Nevertheless it had been a rather unreasonable choice to use it for a flight to Wanderer. The fact remained that the *Ironduke* was a thousand times safer against all eventualities.

THE MAN WITH TWO FACES

This was what Alkher and Nolinov were discussing in low tones at the moment. That the Chief had gone to his cabin shortly after their departure from Pluto did not seem to be unusual. But how could they have known that just now the man they took to be Perry Rhodan preferred not to have anyone around him?

Thomas Cardif was mentally weighing the probability of actually discovering on Wanderer what his father's knowledge told him he was supposed to find on the artificial planet—a relatively immortal being who in some indescribable form represented a combined race of intelligences, discarnate yet possessed of the incalculable knowledge of a people who in eons past had once ruled the galaxy.

With sober logic he evaluated his situation and his plan.

He thought of the hypnotic operation on Okul during which Perry Rhodan was forced to surrender his knowledge and faculties to him, Thomas Cardif. But this transference had not been 100% complete. Cardif's inner ego had retained the upper hand and this represented his greatest danger in the game he was playing in the Sol System. In this respect he was his own worst enemy.

This much he knew but he did not know what would happen when he faced the being on Wanderer and asked for the cell activators.

He tried to analyze his inner state of readiness for the ordeal, searching for any areas of uncertainty, but the longer he searched the more reassured he became. So far the paranormal tracers and telepaths hadn't been able to recognize his camouflage. They still took him for Rhodan and it was this certainty alone that would give him

THE MAN WITH TWO FACES

the full self-assurance he'd need to face the creature on Wanderer.

Thomas Cardif lay on his bunk like a daydreamer. His attitude was relaxed. Nothing in his outward appearance revealed the ingenious psychopath who was forging a plan that would cost his father his life and free him, Cardif, of his dependence upon the Antis.

He hated his father just as much as he had more than 60 years ago. To him the First Administrator was not his father, merely his procreator, and he was the man who had intentionally sent his mother to her death. It was true! Of this he was convinced and any claim to the contrary was a lie invented to protect Rhodan. How often he had searched thru the mental patterns absorbed from Rhodan for thoughtt impulses connected with his mother! None had been found! But for Thomas Cardif there was an explanation for it: Perry Rhodan had given himself hypnotic treatments, no doubt, in order to erase from memory the fact that he had murdered the Arkonide princess Thora!

Of course Cardif failed to realize that such a thought pattern would have had to be transferred to him as well. If his theory were true he would have been aware of Rhodan's intent to submit to such a treatment.

An announcement from the control room startled him. It was Nolinov: "Sir, transition in 3 minutes 30 seconds. This is the last jump."

The real Rhodan would have acknowledged the information with a word of thanks but Perry Rhodan was a naturally born leader of men who knew how to handle his co-workers in order to inspire them to their greatest efforts. Rhodan's double had no such faculty.

THE MAN WITH TWO FACES

In the control room Nolinov glanced at Brazo significantly. "Well, old buddy," he asked casually, "what do you make of the Old Man's mood? I've flown some more cheerful types in my time!"

Brazo wasn't ready to quite conform to Nolinov's opinion. "Don't forget what the Chief went thru on Okul. He only has one son, you know, and when something like that happens to a father, even the strongest man is liable to come away with a few psychological scars."

Nolinov nodded his agreement but he had certain reservations. "That could happen if Perry Rhodan were any ordinary man, like you are me. But he's not. He happens to be the man who built up the Solar Imperium! No, Brazo, a few scars maybe—but not a crack in the old armament like this. I don't trust this ... this whatchmacallit? No matter. Call it shock treatment. I think it went haywire somewhere and if you asked me to lay my money on it I'd bet that his reason for going to Wanderer is to get some real inside advice concerning his condition."

Brazo Alkher looked at his stocky companion in some surprise but he did not have time to make any further comments. The hypertransition jump was due in 5 seconds. The countdown was racing toward the zero mark.

They both strapped themselves in. Zero arrived. The transition followed, accompanied by its process of dematerialization. Then came rematerialization and the men in the I-109 felt the pulling pains that were typical of this type of travel—especially in the area of the neck. The 2 young officers groaned aloud and shook off the last of the shock effects, finally turning their full attention to the gallery of viewscrens before them. They noticed a section of space that seemed to be empty of stars for a distance of at least 5 light-years.

"Did we take a wrong turn, Brazo?" asked Nolinov with a worried frown.

Alkher was already calling for a readout from the ship's positronics in regard to their galactic position. In the same minute the computer chucked out a strip of punched tape. Both men could read the coded symbols as tho they were in normal print.

"We made it, alright," muttered Nolinov, dumbfounded.

"That's the way it always is when you come out in *front* of Wanderer. Normally that synthetic planet can neither be seen nor traced. Hang on, Stant, I'm advising the Chief."

"I'm coming," was Cardif-Rhodan's curt reply.

In his cabin, Cardif got up and stretched himself, after which he took a long, deep breath. He now prepared himself to take the most dangerous step of his life. It was a thing he must do if he didn't want to be under threat from the Antis all his life because of this Perry Rhodan role they had superimposed upon him. If he wanted to cut the strings of the puppet he had to make the gamble.

When he finally left his cabin all sense of anxiety had left him. He was convinced that he could even fool *It!*

* * * *

They had held their breaths when the space-jet flew thru the gap in the energy screen surrounding the synthetic world. Even Cardif was strained to control himself when it suddenly appeared beneath them: Wanderer, planet of immortality!

THE MAN WITH TWO FACES

It was not a planet in the normal sense. It was actually a vast disc, 600 kilometers wide, above which the bell-shaped defense screen arched invisibly. The extensive disc below them contained every aspect of beauty that was to be found in the cosmos. Brazo Alkher and Stant Nolinov would have preferred to look at this miracle for hours on end but they were under the Chief's orders to fly toward a circular clearing, 2 km wide, on the edge of which stood a slender, fragile-looking spire that towered more than 2300 meters into the artificial blue sky.

This was the doman of *It* or *Him*—who had lived here for unknown eons of time!

Just before the gap had appeared in the energy screen, Thomas Cardif had heard from *It*. He heard a voice inside him saying: *Perry Rhodan, do you wish to come to me?*

And before Cardif could free himself from the impact of the strange contact, the inner voice sounded forth again: *I am pleased to see you once more. You seem very desirous of visiting me. But were you not here but a few moments ago?*

Rhodan's transferred knowledge enabled Cardif to realize what the collective entitity meant by *a few moments*. *He* or *It* had a different time concept. What represented decades to humans was for *Him* but a matter of moments.

And now the voice remained silent even as the I-109 made a light landing in the circular area before the slender tower. Cardif stood behind the other 2 men and looked over their heads at the viewscreen gallery. Rhodan's knowledge enabled him to understand what he saw. Nothing here was strange to him. He even knew

THE MAN WITH TWO FACES

where he was supposed to go. The last rumble of the engines died out. Alkhr and Nolinov had shut the ship down.

"Wait here for me, gentlemen," they heard the Chief say behind them. "I am going alone."

They watched him in silence as he traversed the radial corridor and came to a stop at the airlock. The hatches swung open and he left the ship dressed as he was, without any form of protection whatever.

Wanderer's gravitational pull measured 0.9 gravs. The conditions here were almost the same as on Earth.

Cardif crossed the clearing and was approaching the tower when he suddenly heard or perceived the equivalent of roaring laughter in his subconscious mind.

Rhodan, I've almost been devoured by boredom! Friend, how happy I am to see you! It is regrettable that I am not in material form so that I might embrace you and slap you on the shoulder!

Once more the peals of laughter resounded in Cardif's subconsciousness but it no longer disconcerted him. *It* had greeted him as Perry Rhodan. *It* had even expressed the desire to clap him on the shoulder!

Abruptly, however, the laughter ceased.

Come closer friend! continued the soundless voice. *What is on your mind? Ah, you know precisely what it is you wish from me: 21 cell activaors with self-selective individual pattern adjustment. I shall stand by my word. You shall have them. You know, of course, how fond I am of being a spectator when the cosmic game of power extends itself into many spheres. Really, Terran, I believe that the time of boredom is past for me.*

The voice fell silent; the laughter became fainter and fainter as tho receding into a great distance and finally

THE MAN WITH TWO FACES

it died out altogether. While the voice had resounded from his subconsciousness, Cardif had not been standing still. He continued exactly as Rhodan would have done if he had been on Wanderer. His borrowed knowledge continued to guide him as he went.

Also he was more confident than ever now that *It* had also been taken in by this ingenious camouflage maneuver. However Cardif did not suspect that in this visit of his to the synthetic planet he had sentenced himself to death.

He was in the great hall of the tower. Here he waited patiently. It took little concentration to keep his thought stream in the same level as father's. He looked about him with an indescribable sense of exultation, yet suppressing curiosity in place of normal interest, like someone who beheld familiar things he had not seen for a long time.

There stood the Physiotron, the unique device which had thus far sustained the life of Rhodan and his closest confidants. Every 62 years they had to come to Wanderer to receive their biological regeneration.

For a long time Cardif had known that Atlan's life expectancy had been made practically unlimited by means of an egg-sized cell activator. Now he had just requested 21 of them from *It* and *It* had given him to understand that they would be furnished.

When he thought of this outrageous deception a mild shudder ran thru him. He had to marshal all his forces of concentration to still the far cry of conscience somewhere in his depths. He coerced his mind, keeping his thoughts in Rhodan's channels, and concentrated on the 21 activators. He even began to feel like Rhodan. He

75

THE MAN WITH TWO FACES

thought on the basis of his father's knowledge and yet his ideations related to *It* were still not correct.

He resolved not to be merely one of those who had to come here every 62 years for a biological cell rejuvenation. He was determined to acquire the kind of youth enjoyed by the Imperator himself, Gonozal VIII. His thoughts revolved around this single point.

He was aware of the fact that *It* possessed an essential sense of humor and that *It* was fond of weaving certain subtle threads into the fabric of things but—

Cardif stared visibly when without warning the voice called again out of the well of his subconsciousness: *Old friend, you know you are giving competition to your own ancient hero Odysseus. A rather fascinating contest which makes me inclined to oblige. Shall I now place the 21st cell activator in the Physiotron and synchronize it to your personal frequency—Perry Rhodan . . . ?"*

Cardif felt the sweat break out on his forehead. *Yes—* he replied mentally. *Adjust the activators!*

He could have sworn he heard some kind of cosmic tittering, which was the only answer. The pause which followed was short because soon the voice echoed again from somewhere within.

You have raised my spirits today. Terran! And I shall pay you in your own coin. Wait outside the hall. Perry Rhodan, when I have tuned the cell activator to you, you will have the other 20.

With a heady and rapturous sense of euphoria such as he had never before experienced, Thomas Cardif turned to leave. It would be less taxing for him to wait outside than in the great closed room. He forced himself not to run. He walked out, sedately and with measured tread, as Rhodan would have done.

THE MAN WITH TWO FACES

Once outside he sensed the mild and pleasant climate of this artificial world. The space-jet was out there only 1 km distant. Lts. Alkher and Nolinov had followed his orders and had not even left the small conrol room of the I-109.

Thomas Cardif's gaze took in the slender lines of the soaring tower. *Done!*— he thought triumphantly. Yet immediately he brought his mind under close control again. This cautious habit was a true hereditary trait from his father, who never took his victories for granted or endangered them by relaxing prematurely.

Still he permitted himself the pleasure of breathing deeply of the tangy air.

But something stirred in the depths of his mind; he thought he heard a haunting echo of whispered words— something about competing with Odysseus . . . Had *It* seen thru him after all? Had his masquerade on Wanderer failed?

But now suddenly his own ego whispered insistently to him, telling him that *It* had not perceived his mask. *It* had merely been amused by the fact that he sought by means of the activator to eliminate the need for coming here every 62 years to obtain the biological cell shower. Because of this little subtlety *It* had compared his cunning with that of the ancient hero of mythology.

Cardif passed a hand over his brow. The tensions fell away from him once more. Again he drew in a deep breath of the scented air.

He waited for *It* to bring him the 21 cell activators.

* * * *

Homunk "heard" the sound of mental laughter. During Rhodan's first visit to Wanderer, this highly advanced

THE MAN WITH TWO FACES

humanoid robot had been created for him. Now Homunk heard *Him,* his master, chuckling in vast amusement.

He had entered the great hall after Thomas Cardif had gone out. *It* did not wish any contact to be made between the two of them. The multiplex entity of Wanderer chose to speak with the humanoid robot in *Its* own fashion. The creature's appearance here probably wasn't necessary but the situation was so grotesque that *It* felt it had to be shared, if only with Homunk.

Thus it was that a mental dialog ensued:

"Homunk, did you recognize him?"

"At once, Master."

"Anyone with even the name of Rhodan amuses me royally, Homunk. These cultural barbarians from the third planet of a ridiculously tiny sun are capable of ingenious ideas which have to be rewarded."

"Master, will you give assistance to the son of Rhodan?"

"If the little swindler is shrewd enough, why shouldn't I? But he still has to prove how clever he is. Perhaps a clever fraud will use an alias effectively for outward appearances but if he's wise he will never attempt to so identify himself in his thoughts."

"Master, will he understand the question you asked him?—about adjusting the 21st activator to the personal frequencies of Rhodan?"

"Homunk, today you disappoint me. Am I Destiny itself? Only fools attempt to sway the Ultimate Omnipotence. This is why I don't even intend to help Rhodan. Whoever dares to risk so much, as he did on Okul, must also pay the price."

THE MAN WITH TWO FACES

"But Master, now both of them are in danger of extinction!"

"I do not deny it, Homunk."

"Master, you are placing Thomas Cardif in the greatest of dangers!"

"Not yet. Before it comes to that I shall warn him, Homunk. I shall give him a very cogent warning. He has absorbed all the knowledge that Rhodan possessed concerning me. When a man dares to operate as Thomas Cardif is doing, then he must be smart enough to work with alien knowledge. But now it is time to remove the cell activator from the Physiotron. Homunk, will you check to see if it is exactly attuned to Perry Rhodan's frequencies—as Thomas Cardif wished it to be?"

"But Master, Cardif is not Rhodan. He was not able to deceive you and me as he did all the others—but the cell activator will be contra-attuned to him!"

"I shall warn him concerning this contra-attunement very clearly when it is time to do so."

"And what will happen with the other 20 activators, Master—the ones which have been requested from Cardif by the priests of Baalol?"

"A little entertainment, Homunk, and a constructive lesson—so that the Antis may clearly understand that no one may trifle with me, especially for evil purposes. But Thomas Cardif intrigues me—however, he must know the proverb of the cheated cheat. In any case, he is not as shrewd as his father."

The strange dialog in the great hall came to an end, followed by more of *Its* delighted laughter. Homunk's brain was electro-organic in composition and functioned on a 6th-dimensional basis. At this point he dared not make any further appeals to *It*. But he was not too wor-

THE MAN WITH TWO FACES

ried. Knowing *It* as well as he did, he knew that Thomas Cardif was still in charge of his own fate and thus he could still determine the future course of his life.

Homunk was still standing at the rear of the great hall as the cell activator came out of the Physiotron. He watched the egg-shaped device as it floated toward he exit door. Attuned to Perry Rhodan's personal frequencies, it was supposed to give the Terran a relative immortality if he wore it next to his body as did Atlan. But Thomas Cardif was *not* Perry Rhodan! Therefore, would the activator fail to work with him? Or would it produce an effect that was only nebulously hinted at by the term contra-attunement?

Homunk continued to watch the hovering activator as it moved slowly along. The amused laughter of *It* was not loud and yet it was vast enough to fill the great hall. *It* was intrigued by this Terran. In all of *Its* long existence, no other intelligence or being of any description had ever attempted to trick *It* but today this had been tried—hence the entiy's merriment.

* * * *

Thomas Cardif was walking toward the space-jet.

He had accomplished it! He was already wearing the activator on his body. Eternal life lay before him. Now it would take a very violent event to kill him. Henceforth he was immune to cell decay. Thru the incomprehensible workings of the egg-shaped device on his chest his worn-out cells would be continuously replenished.

He had actually pulled it off! Nevertheless he managed to keep his triumphant feelings under control. He was still on Wanderer. There was still danger that *It* might see thru his ruse. Altho the entity was silent now,

THE MAN WITH TWO FACES

It had said goodby to him when he had put on the activator and concealed it under his uniform.

Perry Rhodan, I have adjusted it exactly to your vibrations; and I was happy to do it, old friend. I am sending the other 20 devices along to you. You will find them in front of your spaceship's airlock. Don't worry about the container they're in. When you will it to open, it will do so. If you will it to remain closed, then no power in the galaxy can reach its contents. Goodby, Rhodan, your visit has given me more pleasure than I've known for a long time!

After that the multiple entity could still be heard laughing in the incomprehensible sphere of *Its* existence. The laughter followed Cardif until he was halfway to the ship, then it ceased abruptly.

Cardif was only 100 meters from the space-jet when he felt a quickening current flow thru his body. It was something he had never experienced before in his life. The activator was working, he thought, and he had to use all the energy he had to keep from falling into a state of blind euphoria. He paused to analyze his sensations and then it became unmistakable. He suddenly felt that he was young; he was charged with a maximum of energy, which freed him from an oppression he had sensed since his arrival on Wanderer.

When he reached the small ramp of the ship there was another surprise. Out of nothing emerged a sphere, perhaps 1½ feet in diameter, which was surrounded by a pale red gow. It floated in the air at the level of his head. Within the sphere he could make out the dark shadows of 20 duplicate cell activators. He stretched out his hand and touched the container's surface. It felt cool but not cold; it seemed heavy but Cardif knew it

THE MAN WITH TWO FACES

was not Rhodan's borrowed knowledge gave him the explanation. It was a time-field attuned to his own impulses and it could only be opened by his own will.

He suddenly understood what the community being had meant when It said: *If you will it to remain closed, then no power in the galaxy can reach its contents.*

When he entered the space-jet's control room there was a lingering smile on his face. Stant Nolinov and Brazo Alkher had decided to relax and have a game of chess. They started to spring to their feet when they saw the Chief but he signaled them an "as you were!" and nodded pleasantly to them.

Somehow he had to keep his triumph under control. At this moment he impressed the 2 young officers as being the Perry Rhodan they had once known, if it were really possible—the Rhodan who was frank and open to all.

"But unfortunately you'll have to break up your game, gentlemen. We're taking off."

Cardif-Rhodan ignored the curious stares of the 2 lieutenants, who couldn't take their eyes from the dimly-glowing sphere at his shoulder. He gave them no explanation for it.

Nolinov and Alkher got up in a hurry and got into their flight seats. Using their panel controls they pulled in the outer ramp and closed the airlock door. The engines started warming up. The peaceful quiet inside the spaceship came to an end. There was a roaring and rumbling and howling. Automatic circuits integrated and synchronized the operation of many pieces of equipment. The main transformer set up a deep bass thrumming. A tremor ran thru the I-109.

The 2 officers had no time to look when they heard

THE MAN WITH TWO FACES

the Chief's footsteps leaving the control room. However, while they were making the last preparations for takeoff, Cardif-Rhodan rejoined them, but this time he was not accompanied by the floating sphere of pale-red light.

"Liftoff!" said Brazo Alkher from habit. Altho he was weapons officer on board the *Ironduke,* like all of his peers he had gone thru a heavy training period at the Solar Space Academy to learn how to pilot space-jets, State-class ships and even cruisers.

The I-109 lifted up easily and described 2 long curves around the lofty tower. Brazo caused the space-jet to sway in its course by way of saying goodby. It was a custom that had quickly become traditional in the Fleet but which could not be indulged in when one was flying the bigger spherical ships.

The I-109 shot upward toward the zenith of the energy screen that arched like a bell above the 600-km discworld of Wanderer.

"There's the gap!" exclaimed Nolinov.

Alkher shoved the engines to maximum power and the I-109 hurtled thru the slot into normal space. The small starship had hardly cleared the barrier before its viewscreens showed emptiness where the opening had been. Nor was there anything to be seen of the hemispherical energy screen itself. In their immediate vicinity the almost starless void appeared as if the mysterious synthetic world called Wanderer had ceased to exist.

Wihout saying a word Cardif-Rhodan again left the control room. He had to be alone so that at last he could enjoy his triumph to its fullest. He, the immortal, had achieved his purpose. As for escaping the clutches of the Antis, he was thru playing games. He had 20 pieces of bait now and they wer foolproof.

THE MAN WITH TWO FACES

He closed his cabin door and sat down in a chair. The pale-red glowing sphere of the time-field hovered in a corner of the room. He finally concentrated on it and thought: *open!*

The sphere floated over to him and came to a stop just a few inches above his lap. An opening appeared in its surface and inside he could see one of the egg-shaped shadowy forms move upward. A cell activator came out of the container and fell into his lap.

He picked it up and examined it from every angle. This device differed only in one respect from the activator he himself was wearing. Here on top of the 2-centimeter slot in its surface was the contact for the automatic frequency adjustment. *It* had especially emphasized that cell activators could not be transferred to another without causing them to cease functioning. Cardif laughed aloud when he thought of this.

"20 chances at eternal life, you priests!" he sneered, and he wished at this moment that he could see their faces.

For much less than 20 activators they would have to pay the price he would demand of them! He wondered why he couldn't force them to do his bidding with only one activator. Eternal life was beyond *any* price, wasn't it?

He shoved the device back thru the slot in the time-field. The glowing sphere closed automatically and, as if it were endowed with an intelligence of its own, it floated back to the corner of the room.

"Done!" exclaimed Thomas Cardif triumphantly.

4/ LONG ARM OF BAALOL

After patriarch Catepan and the other Traders had been put thru several hours of cross-examination there was nothing much left to be done on board the *Ironduke*.

Initially the Terrans had been pretty rough with the Springers but that was understandable because no one had forgotten the calamity that had been brought to the galaxy thru Thomas Cardif and the Antis. The death of millions of narcotics addicts was attributed to these antimutants who called themselves "priests".

Allan D. Mercant had conducted the hearing. This was his proper place and forte and with the help of three Solar Intelligence agents who had been based on Pluto it had been possible to get thru the interrogations with a maximum of efficiency.

Patriarch Catepan swore by the gods of Arkon that he hadn't the slightest suspicion that the man Rhodan had shot was a servant of Baalol. No one believed him at first but when 3 hours had gone by and every single Trader from the Pluto base had been mentally scanned by telepaths it became apparent that Catepan had not been lying.

However the surprise was yet to come.

The hearings had ended, the Springers had long since been sent back to their own settlement and the members of top command were asleep in their cabins when the latter were suddenly awarkened by an emergency alert from the *Ironduke's* medical department.

Bell rolled from his bunk with a few typical expletives,

THE MAN WITH TWO FACES

hastily threw his clothes on and dashed to the main ship's clinic station. In one of the lateral antigrav shafts he overtook Mercant, who also knew nothing more than the fact that he'd been startled out of some much-needed sleep.

Dr. Pinter was in the clinic to receive them. Standing beside him was the *Ironduke's* commander, Jefe Claudrin. This was not so unusual but it was another matter to see Jac Hannibal here, who was a specialist in hypercom equipment. Bell and Mercant glanced at each other significantly.

"Something's making me think of our good old Tiff about now," muttered Bell.

"I had the same idea," Mercant confessed.

The man they referred to was Gen. Julian Tifflor, who was known to his friends as Tiff, and Rhodan himself usually called him that. As a cadet in his earlier days he had been known also as the Cosmic Decoy and as such he had performed seemingly miraculous services. But all this had been due to a micro-hypercom tracer transmitter that had been planted in him surgically and which he still carried in his body to this day.

This locator-beacon transmitter had a range of several light-years and in its time it had often served as a trail-marker for Rhodan which brought him unerringly to the center of action. By this means he had been able to make split-second decisions at the last moment, enabling him to strike at the right place with all the forces at his command.

But the other men present were not able to interpret the brief exchange between Bell and Mercant because in the days of of the Cosmic Decoy operation they had not been alive.

THE MAN WITH TWO FACES

"May I ask you gentlemen to follow me into the laboratory?" said Dr. Pinter.

They let him lead the way. It was Bell's first visit here. He didn't like anything that smelled like hospitals, clinics or sick bays, having always felt an aversion for all such institutions.

"Please have a seat," invited Dr. Pinter.

"Thanks, we'll stand," replied Bell. "I'd just as soon not be here any longer than necessary. What's up?"

Hypercom specialist Hannibal went over to an instrument table and picked up a pair of tweezers. On a glass plate lay a pea-sized obect. Hannibal picked this up with the tweezers and held it for everyone to see. "This, gentlemen, is a type of hyper-transmitter you don't see every day. It isn't just because it has a range of more than 50 light-years: this little technological miracle uses the human eardrum as its microphone. And there's one little problem with that: the dead antimutant's tympanic membrane continued to be responsive about 2 hours after he died. This main capsule was embedded in the muscles of his upper left arm and it was able to pick up every word spoken in the vicinity of the body during that space of time. Unfortunately the device was only discovered about 3 hours ago. Meanwhile I needed the 3 hours to figure out how it worked. Do you wish to see this, Mr. Bell?"

Bell didn't need to see it. He had something new to worry about. He was thinking of Rhodan's flight to the synthetic world Wanderer. He tried in vain to remember what might have been mentioned in the presence of the dead man. Certainly somebody must have mentioned that the First Administrator was on his way there in a space-jet.

THE MAN WITH TWO FACES

Mercant must have had the same idea because he tugged at Bell's sleeve. "Let's go!" he said in low tones.

Jefe Claudrin had noticed the swift interchange and looked at the two of them questioningly. When Mercant nodded to him he got the message and followed them. Hannibal watched them go, in some disappointment, but Bell stopped at the door and turned around.

"Thanks very much, Hannibal," he called to him. "I think we may all be indebted to you." Then to Dr. Pinter: "Who located that infernal gadget in the Anti's arm?"

"I did," replied the doctor modestly.

Bell gave him a significant nod of appreciation.

While en route to Mercant's quarters, Bell was already into the problem. "I don't see how it's possible that our

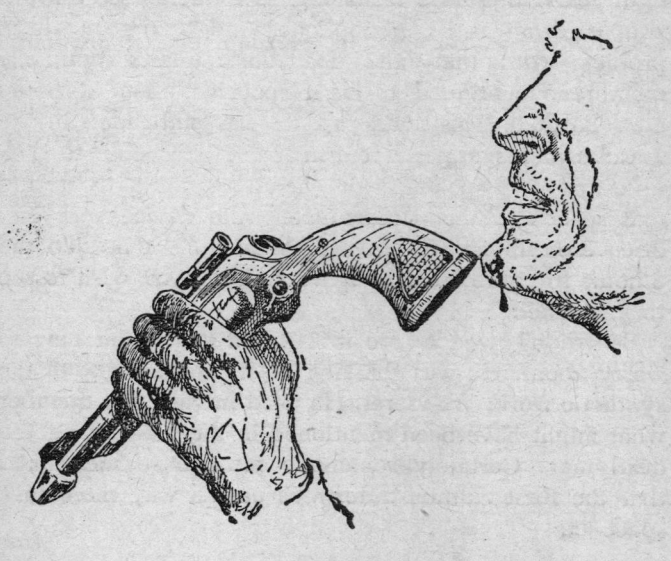

THE MAN WITH TWO FACES

own Com Central and the main Pluto base didn't pick up that transmission. Ordinarily that kind of equipment can hear a butterfly burp!"

"Have you forgotten the Swoons, Bell?" Mercant reminded him.

"Don't tell me those pickle people on Earth and Mars are working with the Antis!"

"I'm not talking about *those* Swoons—I'm referring to the cucumber people on their home planet, and if they're the ones who constructed that super-powerful hyper-transmitter, I wouldn't be surprised if it worked on a pulse-burst principle. You know that any coded pulse-bursts of less than a nano-second's duration can bypass our signal-trace screens.'

"Now *that's* a cheerful outlook! And what's going to happen to the Chief if it hasn't happened already? Are you deliberately avoiding that question—playing ostrich or something?"

Mercant gave him a thin smile. "You seem to forget about Lts. Nolinov and Alkher. The Chief couldn't have selected a better flight team. If anything had happened by now on that space-jet, or if they had run into any danger, we would have at least gotten a distress signal. We're all well aware of what a lightning bolt that Alkher can be."

"Let's hope he still has the old zap on *this* trip!"

Meanwhile they had arrived in front of Mercant's door and Mercant stopped suddenly to look at Bell closely. When Reginald Bell the optimist became pessimistic, something of an unexpected and unpleasant nature was likely to happen. Both of them checked their watches.

"Well anyway, maybe we can catch another 4 hours

of shuteye," commented Bell. He yawned and said goodnight.

"Good night, what's left of it," said the Solar Marshal, and he went into his cabin.

Altho he went to bed, sleep did not come to him. His thoughts continued to revolve around the Chief. And the longer he concerned himself with Perry Rhodan the more uneasy he became.

He stared into the surrounding darkness, which did not prevent him from forming a mental picture of Rhodan's face. He was familiar with every feature of that face and yet now as he looked at its image in memory he thought he detected something strange. But in what respect it was strange he could not say. He only sensed it and then his thoughts wandered off on the wrong course. Without being aware of it he had missed seeing a logical conclusion: he had failed to consider the validity of its instincts.

Solar Marshal Mercant had lost all sense of time and he did not know how long he had lain there brooding alone in the dark when the *Ironduke*'s sirens startled him. Their shrieking clamor announced an emergency, Condition 1.

* * * *

Space-jet I-109 was traveling at more than half speol but no attempt was being made yet to go into transition. Cardif-Rhodan had called thru on the intercom and given an order to make the jump when they had reached 0.99 light-speed.

An order from the Chief was law to these young officers yet it could be seen in their worried expressions that

THE MAN WITH TWO FACES

they were not personally in agreement with this instruction.

Nolinov turned to Alkher. "Buddy, do you have any idea how far we are from our nearest patrol cruiser?"

"Not a fogno*. If you want to know, ask the positronicon."

"Too much trouble," Nolinov grinned. He was kidding, of course: he had only to swing his chair around to face the computer console. He knew that in a matter of secons the positronic brain could shoot out a coded tape that would tell him where the nearest cruiser of the Solar Fleet was located.

The space-jet's velocity continued to increase. Brazo Alkher took a look at the tracking board. Everything zero. Before and behind them, to the right and left of them, nothing but empty space, if one were to discount some very distant stars. Next, Alkher inspected the weapons board.

"What are you doing there?" asked Nolinov, mildly curious.

To Alkher, all types of weapons controls were familiar enough to operate in his sleep. He didn't have to even look at the switch panel to see what he was doing. "One never knows, Stant—and it won't hurt at all while we're still not at top speed to dump one of the power bank outputs into the weapons system. Man, every time I'm sitting in one of these nut shells I'm always happy to remember the kind of armament these space-jets carry!"

"I guess it takes a weapons type like you to work up enthusiasm. I'm in terrible awe of every kind of energy gun. I can still remember my first sharp-shooting run at

*22d Century Contraction For "Foggiest Notion".

THE MAN WITH TWO FACES

the Academy. Man, did my trainer ever make cannibal stew out of me**!"

"What kind of boner did you pull?" Alkher deftly depressed the last contact for his weapons setup.

"What do you think, when a cadet's in the middle of training? We were flying around in the asteroid belt and my target was a big chunk of rock that measured 300 meters in diameter. It might have gone alright if there hadn't been an asteroid in back of it, 10 or 12 kilometers or so, and I think it was maybe 40 km's wide. Well, being all anxious and trigger-happy, guess what I hit?"

Alkher shouted suddenly and Nolinov's reveries were ended. The hypersensor had flashed to life. Simultaneously a gigantic, cylindrical spaceship emerged from the void. The space-jet's automatic magnification system brought the ship in close on the screens so that the ponderous cylinder with its rounded ends seemed to loom directly before them and yet they were separated by a million kilometers. It was a distance, however, which meant litte at 0.60 light-speed.

In the I-109 three sirens sounded the alarm.

And instantly Brazo Alkher became another person. All he could see was the unkown ship racing toward the space-jet. His hand had reached out for the synchro-switch that would flick them into transition but in a split-second decision went past it. He had caught the flash of a heavy energy beam from the long-ship, which moved his hand at once to the weapons board. With the other hand he hit the over-ride on the engines. The propulsion system thundered in response and the alien beam missed the space-jet by several thousand km.

**Chew Me Out.

THE MAN WITH TWO FACES

"I'll take over!" came Nolinov's voice, hard and flat. In a lightning cross-switch of the dual controls he was in charge of the flight.

Alkher had both hands free for his weapons board. It had all happened in fractions of seconds and now Alkher leaned into the battle in earnest. A long-ship was out to get them! That shot had been meant for the Chief!

In this same instant the red-call button sank into the panel. Being tied to the ship's computer, the positronic circuits immediately determined the I-109's galectic position and the powerful hypercom transmitter blasted a distress call into the void.

Even as this happened, Brazo Alkher fired a burst from his 3 impulse cannons. The chance course maneuver the long-ship was making resulted in more damage than was anticipated. Instead of hitting the blunt bow of the vessel as intended, Alkher's shots burned into the enemy hull in the propulsion area.

Then both ships had passed each other.

"Merk!"* barked Alkher in a tone that could not be contradicted.

Nolinov, however, could not have contradicted if he had wanted to. The instruments revealed the reason, they also indicated the identity of the attacker.

Antis!

The power banks of the I-109 were putting out energy as before but with no effect. The servants of Baalol had placed a mental force field around the small but supercharged power installations of the I-109!

Alkher and Nolinov were thus cut off from their engines and power sources. The energy being delivered

*Scram

THE MAN WITH TWO FACES

could only build itself up inside the mental forcefield. If they didn' shut down quickly they could reach a critical point and turn into a bomb.

Nolinov acted. The main switch slammed to zero. Then he man they took for their Chief came running ino the control room.

"Antis, sir!" announced Alkher, and he pointed wearily to the viewscreens. The great long-ship was curving back toward them.

"Antis—?" Cardif-Rhodan blurted out. His eyes were fixed on the screens.

"Sir," added Alkher unsuspectingly, "I think I was able to get out a distress call!"

Thomas Cardif went rigid, momentarily jarred out of control by the thought of a distress call now. "What—?!" he shouted at Alkher. "You mean—over hypercom, to the Fleet?" Even as he spoke this last word he was aware of his slip.

"Sir?" Brazo Alkher could say no more, merely staring at him dumbfoundedly.

"Oh, yes—fine, Alkher," Cardif answered, attempting to get himself back on course. "But how do you know we are dealing with the Antis?"

"Sir . . ." The young lieutenant's amazement was in his voice as well now. "Can't you hear? We had to cut off the engines to keep from blowing up. The Antis have thrown a mental shield around the power and propulsion sections. Not even a radiation particle can get out—"

"Thomas Cardif cut in harshly. "I don't believe I need a lecture on it!" he said coldly, whereupon he turned and went out of the control room.

"Broth-*er* . . !" Nolinov exclaimed. "What's happened to *him?!*"

THE MAN WITH TWO FACES

Disheartened by the Chief's unjustifiable retort, Alkher waved off the question. "How would I know?" But his eyes were on happenings outside. "There! They've put a tractor beam on us—we're being pulled in! Why in the devil didn't I just blast straight into their engine section in the first place? There are no holds barred with pirates!"

At present there was nothing that could change their situation. The only hope they had was the Solar Fleet, provided that the hypercom distress call was beamed from their antenna. As Alkher switched the positronicon to emergency power and prepared to ask it something, a shadow beside him made him look up.

It was the Chief, whose tone was as cutting as before. "What are you trying to find out, Alkher?"

"I've just keyed in a question, sir, to see if our hypercall went out . . ."

"And?"

The Chief's ton was peremptory, which Alkher also swallowed, but it was costing him an effort now to remain calm and civil. "Its signal is positive, sir. Our call was sent . . ."

"We're going in!" exclaimed Nolinov, pointing to the screens.

The viewscreens revealed that the I-109 was entering a large hangar lock on board the Anti ship. Cardif-Rhodan had leaned closer to the screen in front of him, taking note o fthe evident hull damage on the other vessel.

"Is that one of your hits, Alkher? You mean you opened fire on them?"

The weapons officer was at a loss to understand such a question. "Of course, sir! Unfortunately I could only

THE MAN WITH TWO FACES

make one pass at them because all I had was just a few seconds."

A sharp jolt ran thru the I-109 as it came to rest inside the alien long-ship. There was a following slight tremor which must have been the closing of the great hangar lock behind them. The panob screens only revealed the interior darkness of the hangar hold for a minute or two. The Antis must have been pumping air back into the vast chamber because when the big room was suddenly flooded with brilliant light they saw a man enter the area and he was not wearing a spacesuit.

Thomas Cardif instantly recognized him: the man who was approaching the space-jet was the high priest Rhobal. Then the I-109's screens went dark.

At last Cardif realized that he had underestimated the Antis. They were not so easily fooled after all. They had evidently anticpated the possibility that he would attempt a reverse extortion by holdng back the activators for bargaining purposes.

He cursed aloud, incautiously.

Simultaneously he berated himself for this further slip. Once more Thomas Cardif had surfaced instead of Rhodan. For even in this situation Rhodan would have remained calm and self-controlled.

Nolinov and Alkher were exchanging glances significantly.

Cardif snapped out an order. "Nolinov, open the airlock!"

"Yessirl"

"And one thing more, gentlemen: in case the Antis aren't aware of our distress call, don't mention it under any circumstances. It may be our only chance." With

THE MAN WITH TWO FACES

that he turned and went out alone. For his meeting with Rhobal he didn't want any witnesses.

Nolinov turned to stare at his companion, who sat in his flight seat as tho in a frozen trance. "Brazo, get hold of yourself! Isn't it bad enough for the Chief to be rocko*?"

Alkher shook his head despairingly. "Can you tell me what's flipped him around so completely?"

"There's only one answer for it—his sickness! I'm ready to lay odds on it. Rhodan is much worse off than any of us thought!"

At this moment the man they still believed to be their Chief was facing Rhobal, who made a bow to him.

"The servants of Baalol are pleased to welcome the First Administrator," said the priest. "May I ask you to follow me?"

Cardif didn't move.

"If you please, Administrator!" repeated the Anti. His gaze moved warily to his right and his left, which forced Cardif to look in the same directions.

Beyond the main light-banks in the far shadows of the large hangar were fighter robots standing shoulder to shoulder. Their ocular systems were focused on the one item they were programmed for—the simple uniform of the First Administrator of the Solar Imperium. Also aligned with his midsection was the dimly-glowing muzzle of every weapon in the room.

As Cardif finally complied, Rhobal almost whispered to him: "I was sure you'd see it my way."

* * * *

*Off His Rocker

THE MAN WITH TWO FACES

While Bell was dashing for the Control Central and the sirens were still in an uproar, the *Ironduke* took off.

The impulse engines thundered in the supercharged ring-bulge as the double circle of telescopic struts pulled back into the spherical hull and hundreds of crewmen hurried to their stations. Many of them shouted questions as they passed each other but no one knew the cause for the alarm. None except 2 men: Reginald Bell, Perry's First Deputy in command, and Solar Marshal Mercant, Chief of Solar Intelligence. They, at least, were closest to the truth in their suspicions.

When Bell rushed into the Control Central he had to wait like everybody else. The takeoff of the *Ironduke* required maximum concentration by the deck-watch crew who were present. Jefe Claudrin's great bulk was bent over his flight panels as he brought his mighty bird into free space. The powerful Epsalian was among the greatest of commanders, having practically been born with a talent for handling the larger fighter ships. His voice of thunder was issuing commands as he worked.

Bell turned as someone stepped to his side and he saw that its was Mercant. An officer hurried out of the Com Room and after a moment of hesitation ran to Claudrin's custom flight seat with a message.

"Thank you!" rumbled the Epsalian.

The communications man came back but stopped to explain to Bell and Mercant: "Distress call from I-109!" Automatic signal but unfortunately the coordinate data wasn't complete!"

If anyone understood what this meant it was Bell. Incomplete coordinates could mean that the ship might

THE MAN WITH TWO FACES

never be found! The ship's positronicon was put to work and the retrieval programming had hardly been finished before the punched-tape readout was there.

"Well, let's have it!" bellowed Claudrin to the head operator. He was a fast mover and demanded the same speed and precision from his men.

"The area of the probable target zone is approximately 180 cubic light-years," announced the technician. "That's a probability value of 73.6%.'

When Bell came up to Claudrin, the Epsalian glanced briefly at him, anticipating his wishes. He shoved the microphone toward him and then went back to his controls.

Bell spoke into the mike: "This is a dispatch to Fleet HQ . . . Following units alerted for action: third heavy cruiser task force; 18th, 19th, and 23rd light cruiser flotilla also release 3 superbattleships for emergency search mission and possible combat. The target areas is . . ."

The incomplete coordinates which had come in over the I-109's signal beam followed Bell added another sentence: "The Administrator is missing in the indicated space sector. Signed: Reginald Bell."

A re-run of the text was channeled thru from the Com Room. Bell wasn't listening. He was staring at the deck. "For somebody out there, something's gone haywire . . ."

"For whom, Mr. Bell?" asked Claudrin.

Bell looked at him in surprise. He was only aware then that he had spoken aloud. "I don't know, Claudrin. I don't even know what made me say that. So when do we slide into semispace?"

Other than the rebuilt *Ralf Torsten,* the *Ironduke* was the only spaceship equippd with linear drive. With this

THE MAN WITH TWO FACES

propulsion system the discomforts of dematerialization and rematerialization were no longer necessary. A compensating converter known as "the Kalup" served to generate a 6th-dimensional forcefield which compensated for the hard and soft radiations of the 4th and 5th dimensions. Only thus was it possible to move in the semi-space zone between the 4th and 5th dimensional universes, where velocities of millions of times the speed of light could be attained and a special 3-D optical sensor never lost sight of the target star while en route.

In a broad sense it was a flight toward visibility. In comparison to the old system of hypertransition the new method was simply beyond evaluation.

But because of the linear drive the *Ironduke* was capable of reaching the targeted space sector much sooner than the other spherical ships of the Fleet, which had to traverse the vast abyss of thousands of light-years in a series of hyper-jumps.

Jefe Claudrin did not allow Bell's question to disconcert him. "No sooner than usual, Mr. Bell," he answered. "Even when the Chief is involved it doesn't pay to take risks."

Claudrin's slightly caustic reply was justified. It was not too long ago that the *Fantasy* had exploded on its flight back from the Blue System. For any responsible commander, that catastrophe was enough of a warning not to experiment with the new propulsion system.

"OK, Claudrin." Bell wasn't in the least offended by the admonishment. "If anything comes up, I'll be in the chart room."

He took Allan D. Mercant with him. En route neither one had anything to say. They avoided having to criti-

THE MAN WITH TWO FACES

cize Perry Rhodan's actions. In the chart room, Maj. Lyon was already sitting before the charts. He made a move to jump to attention as the 2 men came in.

"As you were, Lyon," Bell told him with a wave of his hand. "I see you're looking over the charts already. Good, we can all see them together..."

After that there were only a few short remarks made now and then as they worked on the stellar data. Finally Bell picked up a magnetic marking stylus and made a circle in a northern part of one of the charts. "That's where we have to look for Rhodan," he said, then glanced at Mercant. "Does that give you any ideas, my friend?"

"Actually, I've noted 2 things, Mr. Bell. So far, our hypersensors haven't picked up any signs of a transition jump. We've had some cases in the past where that has happened, when 2 ships in separate locations have made a hytrans at the same time. There's a blanking or heterodyning effect where the weaker transition is damped out by the other one.

"That's one thing; the other has to do with the spacejet's hypercom distress call. Hypercom transmission isn't subject to the type of interference that often gives us trouble in normal communication, so there's only one explanation for those garbled coordinates: antimutants!"

"Unfortunately we're both in complete agreement!" said Bell grimly. "And my circle on the chart shows where we have to look for Rhodan. But one thing I don't get, Mercant: why didn't the Chief go into transition immediately after leaving Wanderer?"

Mercant's answer was a cautious one. "He may have been attacked just after he left Wanderer but from our

THE MAN WITH TWO FACES

position we can only conjecture, Mr. Bell. We still don't know anything. This enormous area of 180 cubic light-years opens up many possibilities."

Maj. Lyon didn't dare to interrupt the conversation so he could only listen attentively.

Bell grunted perplexedly. "If Perry were only his old self we would be sure of what he might have done after leaving Wanderer. But in a case like this .. ?"

It was an unmistakable confession that Bell was stumped. He threw the marker onto the chart. "Alright," he said, somewhat irritated, "180 cubic light-years is one big chunk of space and even if that sector is fortunately thinned out as far as stars are concerned we'd still be dealing with an unknown quantity of suns. If I keep following the logic of it I'll start counting confetti*."

"I'm almost ahead of you in that department, Mr. Bell," commented Mercant dryly.

Bell couldn't control his temper. He banged the chart table with his fist. "What the devil was Perry trying to do? I'd like to take all those doctors that recommended that shock therapy and . . . and send them to Siberia!"

Mercant smiled ironically. "Siberia has become a summer playground. If I ever retire I'd like to spend my doddering old days somewhere in the tundra. Are you trying to give the doctors a bonus, Mr. Bell?"

"So then you're convinced that this whole bag of snakes is due to a fluke in those shock treatments?"

"Mr. Bell, is there any other explanation for Rhodan's strange behavior? And then there's the death of that Anti at the Trader base . . . I can't get that out of my mind. I had a very good look at that priest and . . ."

*Go Nuts

102

THE MAN WITH TWO FACES

Bell stared at him, curious that he had stopped but forgetting that Maj. Lyon was seated beside them. "Murder?" he asked with a note of anxiety.

"You might put an exclamation mark after that word, Mr. B . . ."Mercant caught himself, realiizng that Lyon was present. He placed a hand on the major's shoulder. and looked at him penetratingly without saying a word.

Lyon met his gaze steadily. "I think I'm going to have to get into this discussion, sir," he said, "but there's really only one statement to make: I'll swear on a stackabye* that the Chief is incapable of murder. There has to be some mistake."

Mercant sighed deeply. "Lyon, I can only hope that you're right." Then he turned to the star map, recalling the galactic coordinates of Wanderer, and pointed out the area. "If you mark Wanderer's position as here, then that makes it the center point of the search area, Mr. Bell. If my hypothesis is correct, then all we'd have to do is draw a line between Wanderer and the Solar System and search along that, with maybe a leeway of 3 light-years on either side of it."

Bell wasn't listening. "Mercant—what were you saying about the Anti?"

The Solar Marshal had been expecting the question. "He was unarmed. His position on the floor was practically an exhibit A—I mean a classical example of a person who has been shot without having been able to even defend himself, much less do any attacking. Rhodan's story about the paperweight is strictly 'no sale'. The blood on it alone is proof of that. Rhodan's chin scratch

*Stack Of Bibles

THE MAN WITH TWO FACES

was too minor for that much blood to have been transferred to the weight. Blood traces are only left on a weapon where a very severe wound is involved."

"Why have you waited until now to tell me all this, Mercant?" asked Bell coldly. Without knowing it he was taking over Rhodan's role more and more. He was in the process of stepping into his friend's shoes as the latter appeared to be more incapable of wearing them.

"Because I've only been able to put it together in the past few hours," Mercant explained. "After coming back from the clinic I couldn't sleep. By the time I heard the sirens . . . Well, it was only then that I had the picture—and now you know."

Maj. Lyon spoke up. "And I don't believe it! The Chief is *not* capable of it!" Bell and Mercant were startled to hear the absolute conviction in his voice.

Finally, Bell answered him. "Major, if it turns out that you're right, then the Solar Marshal and I won't deserve to call Perry Rhodan our friend."

* * * *

Nolinov and Alkher heard the heavy footsteps of robots and they knew what was next.

Nolinov unbuckled his seat belt and quipped sarcastically, "Here comes our furlough, sailor—maybe a permanent one!"

Alkher also unbuckled himself. They were standing unarmed by their flight seats when the first towering robot entered, to be followed by 4 more of the powerful fighting machines.

"Come with me!" ordered the one who had entered first. The thing's weapons held steadily on both the Terrans.

THE MAN WITH TWO FACES

With their positronic escort, the 2 men left the spacejet. The disc-shaped vessel was surrounded by robots but they opened a narrow aisle for them to pass thru the cordon. The Terrans followed the Colossus who had come for them.

When Nolinov tried to speak to Alkher, the metallic voice rattled back at him: "No conversations!"

Nolinov shut up. He knew that robots operated according to their programs and programs had no feelings. He had no intention of committing suicide.

They had no chance to escape and hide somewhere in the big cylindrical spaceship. When they came inside onto the main deck, toward the machine room section they saw groups of men talking excitedly. An uneasiness buzzed thru the ship and shouts were heard. Something about a fire that had not yet been brought under control.

Brazo Alkher smiled faintly, happy to realize that his triple beam shot had caused such damage where it counted. This fact improved their whole situation. By now the Solar Fleet must be on its way to this area, he thought, and it shouldn't be any problem to capture the Antis' crippled long-ship.

Suddenly a heavy blast was heard thruout the vessel, which was almost 1000 feet long. The shuddering had not yet subsided in the floor-plates before sirens began to howl. The various excited groups they had seen scattered now in every direction. The Antis running past them paid no attention to the Terrans. Panic was on the faces of the priests of Baalol.

Nolinov grinned unabashedly and his eyes gleamed when he saw the consternation the sirens were causing. But they were suddenly gripped hard by the robot. A cabin door opened and the two of them were uncere-

THE MAN WITH TWO FACES

moniously tossed inside. By the time they got up again, the door was shut behind them. In some perplexity they looked about them.

"Those robots are real friendly!" muttered Nolinov. He made another check to make sure they were alone in the cabin.

Another grinding jolt struck the vessel's entire frame but this blast was not as strong as the first one. The howl of the sirens continued.

"Congratulations, old buddy!" said Nolinov in grim satisfaction. "You hit these pirates where it hurts."

Alkher modestly shrugged off the compliment. "It was an accident.

Just as I fired, they started a course change, so instead of giving their faces a tan I tanned their toms* for them."

"One of these days you're going to die of modesty," grunted Stant. He was still looking about in the well-furnished cabin. "We need something to break that door open with. You see anything that might be handy, sailor?"

"You mean you want to make a try to escape without the Chief?" asked Alkher testily.

"If that's the only way, yes!" came the unhesitating reply.

"I dont go for it, Stant. We'd do the Chief and ourselves more good if we could pull off a little more demolition in their power and engine sections. Every minute we can delay them here betters our chances. Don't forget our distress call!"

Meanwhile, Alkher happened to place his hand on the door handle. Without thinking about it he turned it and

* Bottoms (As Buttocks Became "Butt")

THE MAN WITH TWO FACES

was shocked to find that it opened! Thru a crack in the door he could see two Antis standing in the passage with their backs to him. He glanced swiftly at Stant, who gave him an answering wink. He was with him.

Soundlessly he swung the door wide open. He took the priest on his right and Nolinov jumped on the other one. The antimutants' outcry was drowned in the howl of the sirens. In the next moment the two Terrans dragged their unconscious victims into the cabin. The door closed by itself and Stant kneeled down beside one of them. Alkher inspected the other priest.

5 minutes later the servants of Baalol lay bound and gagged in the adjoining bathroom. Nolinov and Alkher had appropriated their clothing, which didn't amount to much. Their disguise wasn't very good but they were counting on the turmoil and panic to cover their masquerade on their way to the machine rooms. There was some feeling of security in the heavy energy weapons they had obtatined.

"All set?" asked Alkher.

"Let 'er rip, old buddy!"

The 2 captives left the cabin and as they moved along the main deck toward the engne rooms no one became suspicious of them. The sirens were still in an uproar and crew members were running everywhere. Far aft in the power and engine sections there were still repeated sounds of explosions. It appeared that the Antis had not yet brought the fire under control.

This was almost too easy, Nolinov was thinking—just as disaster emerged from a cabin in the form of a robot.

5/ DAY OF THE ANTI-RHODAN

Thomas Cardif thought that his luck had run out as he looked around the circle of fanatic priests. Even Rhobal the high priest was no longer friendly to him. They were standing around him since he was the only one in the large cabin who had been told to take a seat.

Rhobal spoke to him in cold, threatening tones. "As Edmond Hugher, you were permitted by Baalol to complete your studies on Aralon. As Edmond Hugher you swore your allegiance to Baalol forever. It is Baalol you have to thank for releasing you from the hypno-block that Arkon forced upon you for 58 years by order of your father. And as Thomas Cardif you again swore that you would be eternally grateful to Baalol. With our help it was possible to put Rhodan out of the way; with our help *you* have become Perry Rhodan! And for all this you still attempt to betray us?

"Cardif, one word from us and the Terrans will rip that mask from your face and your game will be at an end! If you don't hand over what you have brought with you from the invisible planet, we shall announce your identity. We would have also revealed your identity if you had managed to get to the Earth with the cell activators. Have you seriously been toying with the idea of trying extortion on us?"

These questions and accusations had been delivered to Cardif like so many hammer blows.

"Where are the cell activators?" asked Rhobal threateningly as he aimed a hypno-beamer at Cardif.

THE MAN WITH TWO FACES

In his helpless rage, Cardif realized that all resistance was useless, yet in the depths of his despair he remembered that the 20 cell activators were sealed in a spherical time-field which could only be opened if he so willed it!

"Rhobal, your 20 activators are in my cabin in the space-jet." Now his voice was calm again. He straightened up like the genuine Rhodan and ignored the hypo-weapon that was aimed at him.

The more than 2 dozen Antis in the room were startled in spite of themselves by the change that had come over him. Suddenly Rhodan's son was radiating that certain essence which had always made his father stand out from the masses.

"Go get them, Rhobal!" he challenged. "I know that you're interested in them only as a matter of course but what's so important, really, about having eternal life? It should mean little to you—or am I wrong? Well? Which of you will receive an activator? Have you already drawn straws among you, to decide?"

He knew these servants of Baalol better than any other Terran. His psychology was deftly applied to play one against the other. Here he was facing the most influential of the Antis. He knew them all and there was not one of them who was free of a greed for power. He knew how each of them had gotten to his present position. Not one of them was prepared to give up an activator willingly.

"Cardif," Rhobal warned him, "you will not succeed in sowing dissension among us, no more than you will succeed in geting away. Do not forget that Perry Rhodan still lives! And he will continue to live as long as you

THE MAN WITH TWO FACES

so that we may always remind you that you are only his son!"

For the firsttime there was a defiant gleam in Cardif's eyes. "Antis!" He spoke derisively as he glared at each of them. "You are not stronger than I! You are planning to take over the Solar Imperium are you? Well, go ahead and try it—without me! Those 300 extra Springer bases

THE MAN WITH TWO FACES

haven't been approved yet. So how are you going to set them up—without me? Neither your agent Banavol nor the Baalol priest you sent to Pluto could force me to the wall!"

Rhobal was quick to accuse him. "Cardif, you murdered Juglun, alias A-thol!"

Cardif-Rhodan answered with a cynical laugh. "Coming from you, Rhobal, that's a strange accusation. Alright, so how shall we proceed in the future? On the basis of equal rights?—or do you still believe you've got the upper hand?" He waited calmly for them to make their decision.

The high priest turned to two of the Antis. "Bring the cell activators from the space-jet!" he ordered.

At that moment the vast spaceship was shaken by another powerful explosion. It brought a faint smile to Cardif's lips.

"Go!' said Rhobal urgently to the 2 priests, who had stopped in sudden fright. His eyes flamed anger as he turned back to Cardif. "If we all blow up because of your space-jet's treacherous attack, you will die with us!" he shouted.

"That I can't change," was Cardif's cold reply.

Then they all waited for the two Baalol servants to return. When the door finally opened, they all expected to see the 2 priests and their coveted booty. Instead of this, a robot pushed Brazo Alkher and Stant Nolinov into the room.

"These two Terrans were on their way to the engine rooms!" blared the metallic voice of the robot. He held his deadly beam weapons aimed directly at Alkher and Nolinov.

The 2 lieutenants waited in vain for a look or a signal

THE MAN WITH TWO FACES

from their chief. The man they had taken for Rhodan looked past them indifferently.

Brazo also saw the Anti who stood in front of the Chief raise his hypno-gun and fire. Then the two lieutenants of the Solar Fleet went into deep hypnosis. They no longer were aware of what was happening to them. They felt nothing at all when, on an order from Rhobal, the robot picked them up and carried them out.

The door hardly closed behind them when an important announcement came over the ship's P.A. system. The fire in the machine rooms had been brought under control. The three main power plants could not be repaired with the equipment available on board. The head engineer did not attempt to gloss over the salient facts:

"Transitions are still possible but I wouldn't like to try more than one at the present time. Any overloads now could cause a complete breakdown of our system. Over and out!"

The priests fell into an excited discussion of their situation. For some minutes they ignored Thomas Cardif until Rhobal composed himself and reminded them that they need not fear for their lives. "We can get away in Cardif's space-jet at any time," he said.

All of them nodded, satisfied, and quickly turned their interest back to their prisoner.

Again the door opened and this time the 2 priests appeared, having returned from their errand. The pale red time-field hovered in the air between them. In its interior could be seen the dark egg-shaped shadows of the cell activators.

The fanatic faces of the Antis were momentarily transfixed by a rapture of awe and wonderment—but the wonderment swiftly transformed itself into greed! There

THE MAN WITH TWO FACES

before them, floating in an alien shell of energy, were 20 keys to eternal lfe!

Even Rhobal's voice trembled as he spoke. "Open that sphere, Cardif!" he demanded.

Thomas Cardif leaned back comfortably in his chair. "Why me? Open it yourself, Rhobal!" He looked the priest straight in the eye.

But during this sudden change of advantage he had failed to see Rhobal adjust the intensity setting of the hypno-gun. The tiny thumbwheel in the butt of the weapon was turned to a minimum charge. Without warning, Rhobal lifted it and fired directly at Cardif. The latter suddenly appeared to be in a trance.

"Cardif!" the priest commanded. "Open the sphere!"

The startled Antis heard Cardif comply: "I will you to open!"

But the faintly glowing sphere refused to open.

What could the Antis know of the multiplex entity on Wanderer? All they knew was restricted to what Cardif had told them.

"Cut it open!" suggested one of the priests. He was so worked up by now that he could hardly speak, so great was his anticipation.

Someone aimed a disintegrator at the energy shell. The beam struck the upper pole of the sphere. Unharmed, the pale red ball hovered in the room as before, only gently swaying from the impact.

"Try a shot from a thermo!" suggested another of the servants of Baalol.

"No!" Rhobal contradicted him because he realized that the sphere would resist any attempt to open it by force. "Only the Terran can open it!"

"But he just tried that!" argued another.

THE MAN WITH TWO FACES

"No he didn't!" the high priest explained impatiently. "He is not himself as long as he's in hypno-shock.'

Rhobol was standing close to the hovering ball. His gaze was still fixed upon the still unobtainable cell activators. It cost him an almost superhuman effort of will to conceal his excitement from the others. Close before him dangled the promise of eternal life! The future was open to him! For him and 19 other servants of Baalol! They would become immortals like Gonozal VIII!

The other priests began to complain and they criticized Rhobal for having used his hypno-gun on Cardif. Their desire for the cell activators was dissolving all consideration of rank; none cared at the moment whether Rhobal was their leader or not. They simply were not going to wait any longer for life eternal! They demanded to have the activators and they even began to shout threats at Rhobal.

But the latter must have anticipated such a possibility. He took a swift look around him and then called out: "Robots!"

The door of an adjoining room flew open to admit 4 combat robots. They took up positions on either side of the doorway and aimed their heavy weapons to the servants of Baalol.

"They are programmed to my commands!" snarled Rhobal. "You will forfeit your life if you attempt anything against me!"

Thomas Cardif had come out of his brief spell of hypnosis by now, and when he saw Rhobal's trouble he laughed, obviously amused.

Like a shot, Rhobal whirled and shouted at him: Open that sphere, Terran, or I'll force you to do it!"

"Those are big words, Rhobal, with nothing behind

114

THE MAN WITH TWO FACES

them," Cardif retorted. He rose to his feet and shoved the Anti aside. Stepping over to the sphere he took hold of it and raised it above his head. "Go ahead, all of you! Feast your eyes on these cell activators which can give you the gift of eternal life! 20 of them are waiting here for you but you will never have them unless I give the mental order, *of my own free will*, for the sphere to open! They lie behind a barrier to our own time, gentlemen. Do you understand that? They are enclosed by a time field and that field will remain closed unless I *feel* like having it open up! Well, Rhobal, do you still dare to antagonize me with your threats?"

He let go of the ball of energy and it remained suspended in the air. There was something peaceful and restful about the pale rose glow of the sphere but it had no effect on the highly excited Antis.

With an exasperating casualness, Cardif went back and sat down in his chair. "Rhobal, are you ready to negotiate with me now or do you still think you can order me around?"

"Negotiate!" exclaimed the other Antis. "Deal with him!"

They were interrupted, however, by a loud announcement over the speaker: "Rhobal, a ship from the Solar Fleet is approaching our position!"

More than 2 dozen Antis stiffened in sudden alarm and consternation. But the man who had usurped Perry Rhodan's position in the Sol System did not rejoice—he cursed inwardly. He could guess the identity of the approaching ship: the *Ironduke!* And he knew that the appearance of the linear-drive spaceship had worsened his situation. Now the Antis would swing back to their old threat of handing him over to the Solar Fleet if he

THE MAN WITH TWO FACES

did not immediately surrender the activators to them.

He looked up. Rhobal was standing directly in front of him. The Anti was grinning at him in triumph.

"Well?" said the priest. He repeated the question with insistent emphasis. "Well, Cardif?"

* * * *

While the *Ironduke* continued to hurtle thru semispace toward its goal, its 3-D sensor optics had not only picked up a spaceship ahead but had also brought out its form and contours on the special viewer. Bell had been waiting for just such a revelation for the past half hour. The 3-dimensional sensor device had been his main hope.

This superimposed tracking system worked on the basis of a parastable, blanketing field compensator which screened the return echo from the effects of 5th-dimensional distortions. Since the 3-D beam expanded with distance and produced a spreading effect that was enhanced by the ship's isolatoin field, it was possible to make observations from semispace and look into the 4-D continuum that lay directly ahead in the straight line of flight.

"Antis!" grunted Bell decisively.

Jefe Claudrin overheard him. "Sir, in 6 or 7 minutes we'll be alongside."

Simultaneously the weird rumbling of the Kalup converter cut off. Claudrin had come out of linear drive because he didn't want the *Ironduke* to race past the alien ship while in semispace. After a few seconds of transitional switchover the impulse engines roared to life. Thus dropped into the normal continuum the *Ironduke* was reduced to a mere 9-tenths the speed of light.

THE MAN WITH TWO FACES

Yet in present quarters this was still far too fast and had to be braked. On the big flight panel the normal velocity readings began to drop rapidly.

Claudrin must have also touched a few alarm buttons. The space-jet hangars were reporting their readiness for action. Then came: "Gun positions on standby!" This was from the Fire Control Central, normally headed by Brazo Alkher.

The Com Room signaled that it was ready.

Claudrin grabbed the microphone. "Transmit data to Fleet units, coordinates and so forth."

"Yessir!" the loudspeaker rattled. "We'll have a confirmation in a few moments!"

Meanwhile Bell had not taken his eyes from the 3-D sensor screen. The big cylindrical ship with its stubby bow and stern configuration was becoming more and more discernible. Being coupled in to the ship's positronicomputer, the tracking system had long since furnished the first range-coordinate data for calculation. From the moment of the *Ironduke's* re-entry into normal space, the main computer had been bombarded with 180 changing variables per second but it was processing them all as tho it were child's play.

In spite of a velocity that was still in the range of half the speed of light, their approach to the alien longship seemed to be imperceptible. Bell was just about to ask for an explanation of this when the C.O. at the positronic board made an announcement. "Enemy vessel is picking up speed!"

Jefe Claudrin responded at once. Once more the impulse engines thunderd to maximum power. The *Ironduke's* spherical hull began to resonate. For some sec-

THE MAN WITH TWO FACES

onds no spoken word could be heard but then as quickly as the thundering had come it suddenly died away.

"That ought to clip off a good minute of approach time!" muttered Claudrin.

Bell shot him a question from his position by the hyper-sensor screen. "Jefe, when do we come into firing range?"

"Alright, my good sir!" bellowed Claudrin, aiming his ire at the computer section's C.O. "Will you kindly give Mr. Bell the time factors? Lieutenant—you and I will have a talk when we get back to Terrania!"

Normally an easy-going person, Jefe Claudrin was a stickler when it came to service performance. His threat concerning the talk with the positronics C.O. was not to be taken lightly.

"Sir!" the lieutenant called to Bell. "Firing range in 330 to 340 seconds if the long-ship doesn't go into transition first. In past 20 second enemy ship has gone into high acceleration!"

Bell hadn't required such precise data but he was already apprehensive that the other ship might get away from them. He could clearly see on the sensor screen that the vessel was leaping ahead at an amazing speed.

Claudrin's voice boomed out again: "Com Central: challenge to alien ship . . . heave to for inspection! Threaten them with firing action!"

Mercant was standing beside Bell. The Solar Marshal only glanced occasionally at the viewscreen but more frequently at his watch. A hundred second had passed since the time-fix had been given.

"100 seconds on your countdown, Mr. Bell . ." He got no farther.

THE MAN WITH TWO FACES

The Com Room made a startling announcement: "Alien vessel *Baa-Lo* threatens to execute Perry Rhodan if our stop order is not retracted at once! This is an ultimatum and we're 17 seconds into their countdown!"

Bell was staring directly at the loudspeaker. "These Antis don't give you a chance to think! ... Com Room, this is Bell! Answer at once: stop order canceled. We agree to stay out of firing range. Ask for a parley!"

Claudrin knew what he had to do. His fighter ship went into a course change as the retro-engines strongly braked the velocity. Under this sudden load the inertial absorbers set up a complaining howl in the depths of the ship. No man in the Control Central paid any heed to it. Not one superfluous word was spoken. Everyone was waiting for another announcement from the speaker, which was due in a matter of second.

But those seconds became an eternity of waiting!

Mercant's eyes were still fixed on his chronometer. "100 second on *their* count ... 105 ... now it's ..."

The expected announcement came thru: "Offer accepted. Ready for parley but Perry Rhodan's life is forfeited if there is the slightest incident. Signed: Rhobal."

"Rhobal!" exclaimed Bell. His brow gleamed with sweat. He would not forget that name till his dying day!

* * * *

Hgh priest Rhobal proved that the title he carried was not unjustified. When the Solar Fleet battleship's presence was announced, he had taken amazingly swift and logical action. He had insisted on having Thomas Cardif next to him so that he could hear every decision he made.

THE MAN WITH TWO FACES

Rhobal realized that he must act within seconds if he and the other priests were not to be lost along with their damaged ship. For many decades it had been known in this part of the galaxy how effectively the Solar Fleet could strike when the situation called for it.

But before the high priest turned his attention back to Cardif he alerted all priests on board, ordering each of them to put his personal forcefield behind the *Baa-Lo's* defense screen so as to reinforce it. During their flight from Lepso it had been shown that not even the silo-thick battle beams of the superbattleships could get thru a screen that had been strengthened by their mental forces. Their only and greatest handicap at the moment was the heavy damage to their engines, which at the most could only deliver a single hyper-transition.

Wordlessly the high priest looked at the man who had been such a major key to their operations for so many years. As Edmond Hugher he had worked for them under a hypno-block and had dedicated his superior medical knowledge to their purposes over a period of almost 5 decades. Not least among his accomplishments had been the discovery of a certain hormone in the glandular systems of the so-called slime diggers of Lepso. This had turned out to be a time-limited but highly effective means of rejuvenation. However it also developed in the human body an addictive poison of very little toxicity.

Thus offered as a rejuvenating liqueur, this cleverly camouflaged poison had come out under the name of Liquitiv on an intergalactic basis and millions of Terrans and Arkonides had become its victims.

Now the two, Anti and Cardif, who had been partners for decades, faced each other as enemies: the extortioner and the extorted.

THE MAN WITH TWO FACES

Rhobal expressed it quite flatly to him: "Cardif, you have your life in your hands!"

"What about the cell activators?" he blurted out. "Do they count for nothing?"

"What value do they have in the present situation?" asked Rhobal. He pointed to the viewscreen. In the abysmal depths of the void was a sharp small point of light: the *Ironduke* . . . waiting. The linear-drive ship had turned on all its searchlights, which was a signal to the Antis on the *Baa-Lo* that the Terran top command wished to parley.

Cardif stood breathing heavily in helpless rage before the priest. It was costing him an almost superhuman effort not to lose control of himself.

"Decide, Thomas Cardif! You have your life in your hands as well as all of our lives but I'll give you the right to make a choice, once you have handed over the 20 cell activators!"

The pale rose spherical time-field hovered in the air nearby.

The ship's Communication Center channeled an outside message directly to the local speaker. Bell's voice was heard, stating his demand for a parley. Only the sound circuits were activated in the receiver system, the picture portion remaining blank. The fact that the viewscreen remained gray was another means of placing Cardif under pressure. He knew that Rhobal's operator could cut in the video portion at any moment unexpectedly, if the situation warranted it, and a scene could be transmitted from the *Baa-Lo* to the men on the *Ironduke* which might make their Chief appear to be suspect.

"Cardif, you heard' what your First Deputy and pos-

THE MAN WITH TWO FACES

sible successor, Reginald Bell, has just demanded. We wish to bring the negotiations to a conclusion quickly. Well, what is your position regarding my demand for the activators? If you refuse, then you and the servants of Baalol are doomed together. If you hand them over, then there'll be nothing in your way as far as leaving this ship is concerned. But once you have gone, don't forget that within 3 days the proposal for an additional 300 Trader bases must be approved. If you fail there, then unfortunately we'll have some other unpleasantries for you!"

Again the speaker blared with a relayed message from outside. Again it was Bell who spoke: "Ahoy spaceship *Baa-Lo!* This is Reginald Bell, First Deputy Administrator! I must advise you that a strong Fleet formation is approaching our present position. Considering the large number of ships, mishaps are possible. In order to avoid such dangers, I suggest our negotiations begin immediately! Standing by for confirmation. Over and out!"

There were 3 combat robots in the back of the room. Their sole object of surveillance was Thomas Cardif. The five other priests who were still present had calmed down in the meantime and had once more submitted to Rhobal's autocratic authority.

"I'll open it!" cried Cardif, forcing himself to yield.

"But don't forget you have to show us how to adjust the activators to our individual frequencies!" Rhobal warned.

Cardif clamped his jaws together and took a seat. The sphere drifted down to his lap and then he concentrated intensively on one thought: *open!*

THE MAN WITH TWO FACES

Instead of merely opening, the pale red time-field ceased to exist. It disappeared into nothingness, permitting the 20 egg-shaped devices to fall into his lap. The priest took 19 of them and shoved them into the copious pocket of his cloak. He handed the 20th one to Cardif. "Now show us how to set it for physical frequency!" Rhobal's voice was adamant and self-assured.

The eyes of Rhodan's son were aflame with hatred yet he finally showed the high priest how simple it was to adjust any of the activators to the frequency of its wearer. Rhobal took the 20th activator from him and also placed it in his pocket.

"You may hail the *Ironduke* and tell them you're on your way, Cardif. However, don't forget to order them to give us a clear transition run with no interference. And would you believe that it's been a distinct pleasure to have you with us on board the *Baa-Lo*?"

Cardif turned his back to him and went over to the local communications terminal. He switched on the viewscreen and waited for it to light up. He finally saw Bell's face, which looked tense and worried.

"I'm coming over in the space-jet, Bell," he said. "Pass the order on to the Fleet units that the Anti ship is not to be hindered, once I leave its airlock. Over and out!"

While he spoke he happened to touch his chest. His fingers contacted the egg-shaped device that he carried against his skin: the 21st activator—that miracle from a superhuman world which also made *him* an immortal!

On the basis of that immortality he was quickly building his new plan—to break the power of the Antis, to eliminate Perry Rhodan forever and to dethrone the self-styled Imperator, Gonozal VIII!

THE MAN WITH TWO FACES

He, Thomas Cardif, was both Terran and Arkonide. He intended to rule both empires.

* * * *

He was racing toward the *Ironduke*. The space-jet's engines were on full-power thrust. The spherical out-

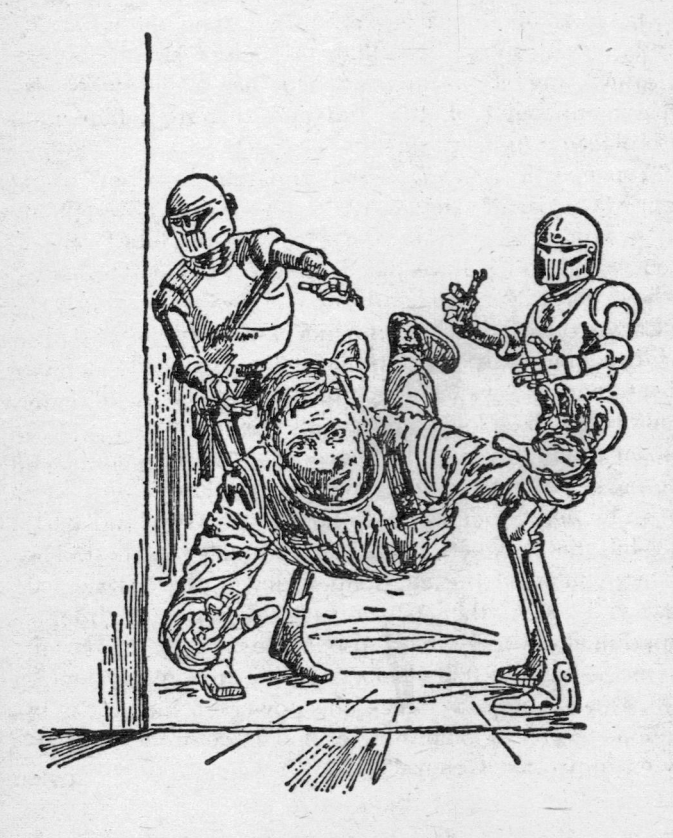

THE MAN WITH TWO FACES

lines of the linear-drive ship were looming rapidly nearer. Cardif was in constant radio contact with the *Ironduke* during the crossing. He had just passed beyond firing range of the *Baa-Lo*, according to his computer.

He suddenly shouted into his microphone: "Attack the long-ship! Alert the Fleet units now approaching! Total destruction!" His voice rang out with rapier impact. The order was irrevocable.

Jefe Claudrin responded immediately. Cardif was already grinning in triumph as he saw how swiftly the 800-meter *Ironduke* leapt out of its free fall course and began to accelerate. The big sphere shot past the space-jet like a phantom within only 50 kilometers. He could see the polar gun turrets open up with all the firepower at their command.

But almost in the same moment his hypersensor reacted. In spite of severe engine damage, the *Baa-Lo* had made a hyper-jump from free fall! Cardif stared at the sensor panel, looking in vain for any coordinate values. The counters rested at zero. And then he understood what had happened. The Antis had been able to make a complete disappearance by use of their mental powers. The space-time continuum failed to react as the *Baa-Lo* made its hyper-transition and re-emerged somewhere among distant stars, back in the normal universe.

A half hour later the I-109 landed in one of the *Ironduke's* space-jet hangars. Minutes later, Cardif-Rhodan entered the Control Central.

"Perry!' shouted Bell exuberantly. He ran both hands thru his stubble of red hair, not knowing how else to express his relief.

Even Mercant's eyes had a high luster as he spoke: "Thank God you are with us again, sir!"

THE MAN WITH TWO FACES

Altho he expressed his compliments he was also raging over the fact that the alien long-ship had escaped him.

It was some time later that Bell casually asked an innocent question: "Where did Nolinov and Alkher go, Perry—back to their stations?"

Cardif-Rhodan had been expecting this question since entering the Control Central. "No," he answered, shaking his head. "The two lieutenants didn't come back with me. I believe they are dead."

In the few second of stunned silence which followed, the chill of outer space seemed to pervade the room.

"Perry, you only *believe* they are dead? You don't know it for sure?" Bell half stuttered the words but he moved closer to the Chief and stared at him. "Come on, Perry—tell me I didn't hear you right! Man, what on earth were you thinking of when you gave that order to destroy the Anti ship?"

"Just what I got thru telling you, Bell!" answered Cardif-Rhodan sharply. His eyes flashed a challenge.

The men in the Control Central held their breaths. All eyes were focussed on just one man: the Chief. But this Perry Rhodan acted like a complete stranger to them. When had he ever left one of his own men in the lurch? And much more to the point—when had he *ever* given an order to attack and destroy when the life of a single one of them was in question?

"Perry!" Bell's voice carried a note of desperation but Cardif-Rhodan cut him off.

"Do you think I wouldn't regret the death of those 2 men? I saw a robot take them away. They seemed to be dead at the time. Unfortunately the Antis wouldn't tell me anything when I asked about Alkher and Nolinov. You know I *could* have simply told you they were dead—

flat out! That would have avoided any misunderstandings."

Bell was visibly shaken. "Perry, you've never thought or operated this way before. I don't understand you. Oh sure! I get most of what happened on Pluto . . . Banavol brought you a report that an Anti was going to show up at the Springer base there. But what I *don't* get was why you took such a highly personal interest in verifying that information. What is Solar Intelligence for?"

Again, Cardif-Rhodan interrupted him. "Solar Intelligence can prove right now whether or not it is still what it was!" As he said this he glanced at Allan D. Mercant.

"What's that supposed to mean?" demanded Bell angrily. That this exchange of words was going on in the Control Central was making him nervous.

"What does it mean?" Cardif-Rhodan's tone expressed bitter scorn. "You will soon find out! It certainly should be interesting to find out why the Antis attacked me and how they knew of my flight to Wanderer. It's not a mere matter of curiosity, Bell—I *will* find out! And now I'd advise you to hang onto yourself when I tell you this: either Stana Nolinov or Brazo Alkher, or both of them, must have advised the Antis of my flight to Wanderer! There is no other answer because the Antis made it quite clear to me that they had been waiting in ambush for the space-jet!"

Behind him, somebody cleared his throat. It was Jefe Claudrin who as commander of the *Ironduke* was directly in charge of the 2 lieutenants whom the Chief was so badly maligning. "Sir . . !" he rumbled warningly —but Cardif-Rhodan also cut him off.

"I didn't ask for your opinion, Claudrin! Mercant, I demand that your organization be put to work at once

THE MAN WITH TWO FACES

on this. In the shortest possible time I want to know where the *Baa-Lo* has landed, where the Antis have gone and whether Alkher and Nolinov are actually dead or alive! Within one week I want to have some satisfactory answers to these questions!"

Mercant's face was expressionless and he ignored Bell's significant glance. The Solar Marshal could not remember ever having heard the Chief give him an assignment in this manner before. Nor had Perry Rhodan ever doubted the ability of Solar Intelligence. "Sir," he remonstrated calmly, "you are asking something almost impossible . . ."

Cardif-Rhodan's imperious hand gesture cut him off. "Possible or impossible, Mercant"—I'm not interested in guesswork! Do you know what's involved here? Do you know what's fallen into the hands of the Antis, thanks to the traitorous help of one of those officers of the Solar Fleet or both of them? Haven't you asked yourselves why the Antis turned me over unconditionally?

"20 cell activators have fallen into their hands! The same tple of cell activator that Atlan wears—but until now he was the *only* possessor of such a device!"

This announcement silenced even Mercant. Bell seemed to be trying desperately to catch his breath. Many of the officers in the Control Central had turned visibly pale. Their Epsalian commander had apparently forgotten the Chief's rough reprimand.

And Cardif-Rhodan stood there triumphantly in their midst. He himself broke the uncanny pall of silence: "Is it understandable now why I issued the order to attack and destroy?"

Thomas Cardif exulted inwardly when he perceived that even Solar Marshal Mercant's attitude was less ac-

THE MAN WITH TWO FACES

cusing. And the underhanded chess play he had made, branding the 2 blameless officers as traitors, was now bearing fruit.

There was only one man present who would not be moved from his own opinion. The thunderous voice of the Epsalian filled the room. "Sir, I beg your pardon but I cannot believe that Alkher or Nolinov betrayed you to the Antis! If that were true, then I'd cease to believe in humanity itself. In that case, you could also call me a traitor to yourself and the Solar Imperium!"

Cardif-Rhodan had allowed the *Ironduke's* commander to finish speaking. Now he walked over to him and laid a hand on his shoulder in a traditional Rhodan gesture. "Claudrin," he asked "can you explain to me then how the Antis knew of my flight to Wanderer? If I have suspected the 2 lieutenants unjustly, then is there someone else or perhaps several others you'd care to suggest, on board this ship, who might have committed this act of treason? And one thing more, Claudrin: how is it that the servants of Baalol asked me about the cell activators as soon as they captured me?"

The commander stared at him with widened eyes and finally shook his ponderous head. "I'm sorry, sir, but not even that is going to convince me that those men could be traitors. Something else has to be involved here which we know nothing about. Maybe Solar Intelligence can come up with an answer."

Cardif-Rhodan did not have a chance to reply.

"Claudrin," said Mercant swiftly, "I'll tell you one thing right now . . . In fact, I'll swear it! Solar Intelligence will furnish that answer—or my name isn't Allan D. Mercant!"

THE SHIP OF THINGS TO COME

"DIE, Kalal! Die!"

It reverberated in his head like an agonized cry and made him utter similar screams of anguish. An invisible power lifted him from his cot and hurled him to the floor, where he remained writhing and shrieking violently.

However he also could feel the pain he suffered as he hit the floor and it was proof for him that he was still alive. He had repulsed the onslaught and remained victorious—victorious over the combined awesome power of the 10 mighty brains.

The mental shield he had created around himself had proved effective. It had withstood the murderous command and hurled it back to its source.

He prepared a message in the code use for radio communication with the friendly nation of Springers. FRIENDS! KALAL ON UTIK REQUESTS YOUR ASSISTANCE. EXTREMELY URGENT! PLEASE COME AT ONCE!

"Dangerous Opponents" . . . "Subterranean Discoveries" . . . "Shocking Surprise" . . . "Violet Flower: Violent Hour"—these are some of the fascinating chapters you will read next in—

WONDERFLOWER OF UTIK
By
Kurt Mahr

Treasured Tales from

THE TIME VAULT

An Ackerman Archival Recovery

THE FACE IN THE MASK
by
Estelle Frye

"A SAVAGE, MAGNIFICENT STORY," said Editor Cele Goldsmith, "which begins where others leave off. *You will remember this story.*"

And she was right.

I have remembered it since 1961, when I first read it.

It was a "First" for Estelle Frye. And, unfortunately, a last. She came to a few meetings of the Los Angeles Science Fantasy Society, became a client of mine from whom I expected a brilliant future, but left town before long . . . and was never heard from again.

Oddly enough, another oneshot female sf author debuted in 1961: Alice Glaser. Some years later the late Rod Serling contacted me to check out her story "The Tunnel", which he was interested in considering for adaptation for TV's *Night Gallery*. I tracked her down, talked to her on the phone—LA to New York—but Serling never entered into negotiation and Alice Glaser . . . died.

I hope Estelle Frye isn't dead. For one thing, there's a reprint check waiting for her at 2495 Glendower Ave., Hollywood/CA 90027. But, for another, I think she's de-

THE MAN WITH TWO FACES

serving of more egoboo for THE FACE IN THE MASK than a single printing and then oblivion.

You will let me know. Did I do right in opening the Time Vault after 15 years and bringing back Ms. Frye's "Face" to the light of day?

Say!

* * * *

John Peel snapped the shaver back in its slot and pulled down his masker. He was late this morning. The Voice gave a melodious whir and said, "You now have ten minutes to catch your car, John." He slid the masker down his cheek, smoothing the pale gray plastic over his face. Halfway down it sputtered and the liquid came out in uneven drops.

Blast! He fumbled for a fresh tube, took a precious minute to refill the masked. Stripped off the right cheek and started over. Sometimes it could be bonded together, but he didn't want to take a chance on being caught in public with a crack showing.

He gave himself an embarrassed grin at the thought. The mirror with its subliminal message flashing, "You are a handsome and virile male," reassured him. He finished masking, then stared at his face again. His eyes, alive in the gray mask, stared back at him, seemed to ask, "Who am I?" His lips parted slightly and he leaned forward as if to listen for the answer, but there was no reply except the message from the mirror repeating itself a thousand times a second.

The Voice, now strident with alarm, said, "You have five minutes to catch your car!"

He whirled and ran into the sleeping room, snatched

THE MAN WITH TWO FACES

up his gray coverall with its gleaming white collar, and threw it on.

It was not until he was on the station platform, surrounded by the grayness of the other masked and coveralled men and the pink that was the women, that he realized that instead of his briefcase of cards he held a piece of toast in his right hand. His stomach, resentful at being left without breakfast, had betrayed him into grabbing the toast from the breakfast slot instead of the card case from its rack.

Oh, well, he thought, *what difference does it make if I don't talk? I never say anything anyway.* Shocked at himself, he glanced hastily at the city mural painted on the walls. The subliminal hidden in the skyline soothed him. "I am going to catch a clean and speedy train to my pleasant place of work,' it said. The tension in his stomach subsided. He saw a woman eyeing the piece of toast and stuck it in his pocket.

Aboard his car he hurried to the men's compartment to eat his toast. As he chewed the dry stuff he wondered resentfully why he should have to hide, though of course he knew it was because chewing might crack his mask. He glanced in his wrist mirror, then went down to the Artists' Car.

Hawkins sat in his usual seat. He nodded at Peel, flipped open his briefcase and pulled out a card reading, "Nice day." ....

Peel nodded uncomfortably. Hawkins clearly expected some response, so Peel cleared his throat and averted his face. Scarcely moving his lips he murmured, "Forgot my cards."

Hawkins' hand dived into the case, came up with a

THE MAN WITH TWO FACES

card reading, "So sorry to hear it. Know how you must feel."

Peel stared out the window at the Painted Forest. He tried to pick out the pine trees he had worked on, but it was impossible with so many others. He felt tired and out of sorts. Why shouldn't a man be able to find the trees he had painted? He purposely kept his eyes from the sky even though he knew the subliminals there would make him feel better. That was the trouble with working for Scenery. When you were onto it all, it took some of the pleasure out of it. He knew the messages by heart: "I'm lucky to have such a good job." "I'm well paid." "I'm happy." At the little country village they changed to: "I'm going to work hard today." "No wasted time." "I'm glad I'll be doing my part."

The waterfall came into sight. *There was something wrong with that fall*, he thought irritably. He wasn't in water himself, but every time he saw that cascade leaping down the rocky cliff he felt vaguely disturbed. He frowned at it till it was out of sight.

He turned to find a small man across the aisle looking steadily at him. Peel's hand strayed over his mask. Was something wrong? Who was the fellow? Why was he watching him?

No matter. Today, he decided, he was going to paint a drooping branch on one of his pines. He could see it in his mind's eye. He would tip the needles ever so slightly brown. After all, trees shouldn't always be straight and green. Why didn't they understand that? Not much, or the inspector would catch it, but just a little. He could see just how it would be. Then he'd be able to spot it from the train, too. For the first time that morning he felt good.

THE MAN WITH TWO FACES

The Car Voice called his station and he got up and went to the exit, brushing past the Security man on duty. It seemed to him that this man, too, stared at him. His right hand felt strangely empty without his card case.

At work he sketched n the pine tree as he had planned. Glanced covertly around, picked up his brown paint and mixed in a touch of gold. Delicately he lengthened a branch, drawing it downward, touching the tips of the needles with golden brown paint. Just a little, to show the branch was dying, the needles ready to fall.

In the mens cafeteria at noon the music was on and the Voice would cut in with announcements: "Bowling teams will practice at 7 P. M." or "We have now had 26 days without an accident!" but still there was a barely audible sibilant undertone. Someone was talking. Peel looked around, but whoever it was wasn't moving his lips. Cards flashed as men held them up to each other.

At his table it was the ball game. "I think the Dogers will win," read Johnsons card. "Want to bet on that?" Martin's card answered. Johnson held up a five dollar bill. The other nodded. Without his cards Peel was out of it.

There was the little fellow who had stared at him on the train, seated with a big burly man. Peel passed them on the way out. The smaller man held up a card, "How's everything going?" Peel shrugged, showed his empty hands.

"I'm Mitchell," the man said in a low voice. "Who are you?"

Peel tried to look away, but both of them were staring at him fixedly, their eyes bright, and his own glance was caught and held. "Peel," he mumbled, then looked around

THE MAN WITH TWO FACES

to see if anyone had noticed him talking. He ducked his head and hurried back to work.

Just before quitting time the supervisor handed him a card: "You're wanted in the office."

There were two of them waiting for him, Security men, their eyes as cold and bleak as their gray coveralls.

The first card read: "You spoke to someone on the train."

Peel turned his face aside. "I forgot my cards."

"Do you forget them often?" the first one asked aloud.

Peel shook his head. *Do many people forget?* he wondered.

"Do you know a man named Barr?"

He shook his head again.

"Are you sure? You were seen with him in the cafeteria."

"Everyone's in the cafeteria," Peel mumbled. "They all look alike."

The second one pounced. "Shouldn't they?"

"No. I mean, yes."

The second one wrote busily on a pad.

"What do you talk about?"

He shrugged. "Nothing."

The two rose; the interview was over. The first one handed him a card. "Remember," it said, "we have ears everywhere."

The lips in the gray masked face parted slightly and he stared straight at Peel as he asked, "Do you want to be declared PARIAH?" Then they were gone.

Peel shuddered. To be PARIAH was to be cut off completely—no one would even give you a card.

He hurried back to work. The gray figures around him

THE MAN WITH TWO FACES

seemed to turn their backs. Had that man on the train—Mitchell—reported him? Peel tried to catch someone's eye, but to no avail.

Running for the car after work, he saw Mitchell again, caught his sleeve.

"Who are you?" he asked in a low, urgent voice.

"Who are *you*?" Mitchell retorted and turned to join the same big man who had been with him in the cafeteria. Together they got on the train.

Peel rode back to the city sunk in gloomy thoughts. Getting off, he made his way to one of the movng sidewalks on each side of the downtown street. The walk was crowded; he had to shoulder his way on. The men and women standing there were silent except for the faint hiss and click of cards being exchanged. Their bodies seemed tense and stiff, and he noticed that most of them would ride to the end of one walk, then transfer to another going back the other way. Like him, they seemed reluctant to go home to their boxy little rooms. At each corner a Speaker was on; music swelled to a crescendo as the corner neared, then dwindled away in the center of the block.

Everyone stared at the lighted shop windows. A display of white-collared gray coveralls blazoned, "Everybody's a white collar worker now!" For the women there were pink tunics, window after window of them. "Be a rosy girl," the message flashed electronically. As far as Peel could see, the women were all obeying; their pink tunics fluttered in the evening breeze.

The card shops were still open. In one window a placard asked: "Why take a chance on saying something yourself? Let a card say it for you." Below was a giant blown-up card showing a woman crying. Printed above the anguished face was the legend: "You forgot our anniversary!"

At the end of the store section Peel stepped off the sidewalk, wandered off afoot. On a side street an old woman approached him, pulled out a tattered card. Holding it before him, she peered up into his face. Her mask was half peeled off, the skin underneath dirty and wrinkled. "Can you spare a dime?" the dog-eared bit of cardboard read.

Instead of revulsion Peel felt pity for the woman and even admiration. How had she kept from being institutionalized?

He thrust a silver dollar into her hand. "Here," he said brusquely. "Enjoy yourself."

She gaped at him, and her tired eyes filmed with tears. "Mister," she said in a hoarse and creaking voice, "you're the first person who's spoken to me in weeks. Aloud, I mean." The tears ran down her cheeks. "You don't know what it means. Thanks for the dollar, that was nice of you—but thanks for talking even more."

"Say," he asked, "do you remember when people used to talk?"

"I'm not that old, but I remember my father used to tell me when he was a boy people spoke right up, said whatever they wanted to. Then..."

A door slamming nearby made them both turn in alarm, and when Peel turned back to the old woman she was gone, already almost out of sight in the gloom as she scuttled up a side street.

He looked back toward the bright streets behind him.

THE MAN WITH TWO FACES

Silhouetted against the light he saw two figures, one small, one large, coming toward him. He hesitated, then plunged on into the darkness.

Ahead of him, light streamed from a doorway. The sign over it read *Vordys Place, Talking and Eating House*. He had heard of them but he'd never been in one. They were not really illegal, but they were on the thin edge and every morning he read of one being raided.

He heard footsteps from the corner and ducked in the door. Inside, the air was heavy with smoke, the tables crowded. He sat down at a small table. Spotlights focused on a small stage and a group of girls came on, dancing. At the end of their dance they pulled off their masks, threw them up in the air. Their faces were painted, chalky white cheeks and red lips. The men in the room roared with approval.

Peel slumped in his chair and drank wine. He stared around through the smoky haze. What kind of people were these who talked, ate in public, watched women unmask? A girl walked up to his table. One of the dancers. With a negligent air she handed him a card: "Want to buy me a drink?"

"Sure," he said.

"Well, look who's talking," she drawled. "I didn't think you were the type." Her eyes were knowing, the lids blue-painted, they eyelashes gilded.

He drank some more wine, the girl drinking too. Her pink tunic clung to her body. Below it, her knees curved softly as if they were boneless under the soft and silken skin.

"You're beautiful," he said "without that damn mask on." His hand reached out to touch her knee.

THE MAN WITH TWO FACES

A sweet smile curved her lips, then froze into a grimace. She barely moved her head, and Peel looked around.

Two figures had paused by the table. "You're Peel, aren't you?" the smaller one asked.

"What do you want?" Peel got to his feet.

"Sit down, let's have a drink together," the big one said.

Peel's mind raced. Were they Security men? He felt knowing and crafty. "Order me a drink," he murmured, "I'll be back in a minute." He walked toward the rear of the room, down the hallway to the toilet, kept going till he came to the kitchen, through it out to the alley.

No one noticed hmi. He raced down the alley, made his way by side streets to the edge of the cty. He was afraid to go back to his apartment.

Nearly every one these days lived in the city in the towering beehive apartments. Great walls of painted scenery surrounded the town and lined the speedways. He found a gap in the wall where a board had crumbled and earth had been dug away. Probably children had played here, had scrambled under the walls to adventure. He wriggled through, stumbled across a weed-grown field to a narrow road. The glow from the city behind lit his way. Here and there he could see abandoned houses slowly decaying. When he was tired he walked over to one of them, pushed open the rotting door and slept on the floor within. He woke in the morning, stiff and sore. His clothes were rumpled, his beard was sprouting against his mask. ....

He wandered on through the countryside till he came to a little shack of weathered gray wood. An old man sat on a bench in front of it. He wore no mask, his hair was long and shaggy. He had a white beard and was

THE MAN WITH TWO FACES

dressed in a shapeless coverall. He was barefooted, his feet gnarled and horny. .. ..

Peel stopped. "Good morning," he said. The words sounded shockingly loud.

The old man opened his mouth. "Are you the Beast from the East?" he asked. His eyes brightened and gleamed.

"I come from the city," Peel said.

"Sodom and Gomorrah," the old man said. He got to his feet, bent to pick up a crooked stick. "Don't come near me."

"Wait," Peel said, "I just want to talk. You don't wear a mask."

"Every man wears a mask," the old man said. "The day will come when they shall be ripped from them and the face of the beast revealed." The shaggy head lowered. "Are you a spy?"

"I'm just a man," Peel said. "Here, I'll take off my mask." He was making the ultimate gesture—here under the open blue sky to unmask, to talk to a stranger. The air was sweet and clear. Peel lifted a hand to his face.

"No," the old man said. He cowered away. "I don't want to see your face. Go away. You're a beast set upon me!"

Peel ripped off his mask. "I'm just a man,' he said again.

But the old man covered his eyes with his hand and brandished wildly with the stick.

"Go away!" he screamed. "Go away!"

Peel turned and walked off. Behind some trees he took out his pocket masker and spread a film of plastic over his face.

He might as well go back; there was nothing for him

out here but decay and madness. He trudged back to the city, scrambled back under the wall, went to his apartment to clean up. He was surprised they weren't there waiting for him.

He wasn't going to sit there and wait. Let them come for him at work. He picked up his card case, caught the train, almost empty at this time of day.

No one spoke to him or passed him a card. He came to the waterfall, looked at it with dull eyes. "Who am I?" he thought suddenly.

As he walked through the locker room a small figure moved to intercept him. At his elbow was the big man, his shadow.

"We've been looking for you," the big man said softly. "My name is Barr. We want to talk to you."

Numbly he let them lead him aside to a corner. "Why me?" he asked.

"We saw you noticed the waterfall," the big man said. "That was my work. Mitchell here is in rocks. And you're in trees."

A week later Peel again watched out the window of the car as it sped toward Scenery. There was the grove of birch trees he'd painted, their white trunks standing out amidst the evergreens. They had calculated they would draw attention.

He transferred his gaze to the other passengers. Hawkins lifted his hand and rubbed it irritably over his face mask. There was a little stir of movement as other hands lifted to faces. The subliminal on the birch grove, installed on the night before by Barr and an inspector from electronics, read, "This mask itches."

Peel smiled secretly. Even the Security man was poking at his cheek.

THE MAN WITH TWO FACES

Further on was the outcropping of limestone, Mitchell's work. "I'd like to talk to somebody," it flashed. There was an anxious stir in the car. No one spoke, but several men pulled out cards, shoved them at their seat mates. A throat was cleared.

New York wasn't built in a day, Peel thought. Tomorrow he'd speak to someone, aloud. Tomorrow, or the next day, he bet they'd answer.

The last secret subliminal was Barr's waterfall. "Who are you?" it asked as the false water poured down the painted cliff.

Peel sat up straighter. *I'm John Peel,* he thought proudly. *John Peel. Myself.*

25 ADVENTURES FROM NOW
You'll encounter the
Beasts of Subterrania

TRIPLANETARY AGENT

By

William B. Ellern
(Author of NEW LENSMAN)

Larry McQueen, the local Triplanetary Secret Service Agent on Mercury and Noel Elliot, a repairman, were at the Bubble's antenna site checking why messages sent to the Triplanetary Patrol weren't being transmitted, when they were captured and taken to the secret pirate base at Mercury's pole. Larry is in constant communication with Bill Howard, his Sector Chief, using a disguised, Service Special ultra-wave communicator. Larry and Noel are on their way to be interrogated when Larry stops to light a cigaret with his Service Special lighter.

Chapter 5

INSIDE THE PIRATE BASE

Larry suddenly gave a cry of pain, threw the lighter away and doubled over. The repairman standing to one side closed his eyes and turned his head away. The guards, not knowing what to expect, drew their guns and looked at the lighter to see what had happened. It went off with a magnesium flash, blinding the guards.

THE MAN WITH TWO FACES

It took Larry less than five seconds to kill them. They took the guns and headed for the warehouse at a casual pace.

"Our first need is personal defense," Larry explained to the repairman. "We can't hope to do anything here to help ourselves unless we have suitable protection and overwhelming weapons. We've probably got about five minutes before the alarm is given, to get ready to protect ourselves."

They ignored the people they met, and were in turn ignored.

They walked into the office of the warehousing operation. "We're new here," Larry began forestalling the obvious questions about the clerk not having seen them before. "In half an hour we've got to go on a mission with Gill and Brandon. They sent us down here to get armor and weapons." The names were those of the men on the hopper that had brought them. In answer to the next question Larry angrily answered. "I don't know anything about projects or charge numbers. All I know is one of the big wheels wants us out of here in a hell of a hurry and we need the equipment." Then he threatened and bullied. Within minutes the materials were being lent until a proper charge number could be found.

"We're going to suit up here," Larry concluded. "It'll be faster than trying to carry that stuff out to the hopper."

They both walked out in full armor, fully armed and pulling a truck with a semi-portable weapon on it.

The alarms went off while they were in the elevator going up to the communications center. When the doors opened Larry looked around. "Hey, you two!" he called to a pair of men waiting for an elevator. "Give us a hand

145

THE MAN WITH TWO FACES

here. We've got to get this gear down to the Communications Center to defend it."

The men looked a little hesitant for a moment.

"I'm not kidding, come on, snap to!" Larry barked. They snapped to.

They wheeled the semi-portable into the communications center and set it up on the tripod facing the door.

"Now get out of here before trouble starts," Larry dismissed the two men. They left hurriedly. Larry turned to the manager, who had come hurrying across the room to see what it was all about.

"Noel, man the gun," Larry commanded the repairman, then turned to the manager, "Who's in charge here?"

"I am."

"Good, is there any way to lock or seal off that door until this emergency is over?"

"Yes, the red button up there next o the door puts up the shield," he answered, pointing to a couple of large colored buttons a little above head level. "The green one turns it off."

Larry walked over and pressed the button. "Is there any other way into here?"

"No."

"Alright," Larry said. "Keep quiet and get everyone over there against that wall or I'll use this."

The manager looked down and saw a gun pointing at his stomach. He turned pale.

Noel had the semi-portable casually turned around and was covering the room. In a few moments everyone in the room was along the wall and covered by the semi-portable.

"OK, now let's go call the Hill on Tellus," Larry said,

THE MAN WITH TWO FACES

and went with the manager over to a visiphone and made the call.

Bill Howard, who had been listening in on the service special communicator, said, "Ask for Evans. The password that will get you in is 'triple E'."

Larry recognized the name as belonging to a member of Samm's general staff.

When Evans' face appeared, he took one look at Larry, and said, "I'm recording this, go ahead."

"There's a pirate base at Mercury's north pole." Larry said without preamble. "We need the *Boise*, now, and any other help you can give us to reduce it." He continued to explain the situation. Evans was busy as he talked. Other faces appeared in the corners of the screen as he added them to receive his call.

When Larry was finished, Evans' orders were simple. "Destroy that communications center and get out of there as fast as you can."

"Alright," Larry announced to the people along the wall. "There's going to be a lot of smoke here in a couple moments. I suggest you all get down on the floor where the air will be a little more breathable. Noel, you heard our orders. Destroy that stuff."

Noel turned the semi-portable on the consoles, visiphones and televisotypes in the room. The beam of vibratory destruction turned them into charred, smoking, melted trash in seconds.

Larry checked the other side of the door with his goggles. There were about five armored figures waiting for them. No heavy weapons yet. Noel's semi-portable could kill or disable them but it couldn't be brought to bear on them fast enough in close quarters to prevent

THE MAN WITH TWO FACES

them from rushing in and overpowering Larry and Noel by sheer weight of numbers.

Larry looked around at side corridors. "Noel, cut an exit over there in the rear wall," he said, pointing.

The semi-portable cut through the wall literally like a hot knife through butter. They loaded the semi-portable back on the truck and headed out the still smoldering wall. At the corner they turned and headed for the main corridor. Ahead several armored figures crossed the intersection on their way to the communications center door.

When they reached the intersection, they unloaded the semi-portable. "Call the elevator," Larry directed, calmly. While Noel headed for the elevators, Larry opened fire. The shields in the pirates' armor could withstand indefinitely the beam from the semi-portable, even pistol fire but Larry switched over to shells. Within seconds the main corridor seemed to be filled with half-kilogram missiles fired from the automatic loading weapon. Larry had no intention of being pursued by someone capable of stopping him.

When the last form was down, Larry stopped. There was the sound of a bell behind him announcing the arrival of one of the elevators. "Get out of the line of fire," Larry shouted as he swiveled the semi-portable around on its base. Noel moved to one side. The doors opened and two men emerged, firing their guns. Larry blew them apart.

Noel held the elevator doors as Larry struggled to get the semi-portable back on the truck. "Can't do it," he finally said. Noel looked around for something to jam the elevator doors open. He finally pulled one of the dead men halfway into the elevator to do it.

THE MAN WITH TWO FACES

They got the semi-portable loaded and into the elevator. Larry pressed the button to go back to the level of the landing dock. The elevator didn't move! Larry looked at the control panel. A piece of shrapnel had smashed through the wall above it and torn up some of the wiring there. There was no quick way to get at the wiring to repair it, even if either of them had known which wires should be connected together.

"Let's try another elevator," Noel suggested.

They got out and called another elevator. As a sudden afterthought Larry used one of his guns to weld shut the stairway door.

The elevator arrived, empty. They muscled the semi-portable into it. And then, again as an afterthought, set it up.

The elevator started down, the wrong way. Larry immediately hit the emergency stop button. "Sometimes this will clear the memory," he said. It didn't. When he released the button they started down again. "Someone down there wants this elevator," he said. "We've got to go down before we can go up."

They went back down to the warehouse level. The doors opened to reveal almost a dozen armored men with three semi-portables on trucks. Noel immediately opened fire. Within half a minute all but one of the armored men were down and the semi-portables were wrecked. The sole survivor had managed to make it to the cover of the cross corridor. It had been more of a slaughter than a battle, even though some of the men had fired back with ineffective handguns. The borrowed armor that Larry and Noel were wearing could easily withstand almost any amount of that kind of abuse.

THE MAN WITH TWO FACES

"We're low on ammo," Noel said. "Can you get a box from one of those semi's? I'll cover you."

Larry fished through the wreckage in the corridor. He found an undamaged box of ammunition, and a number of grenades which he transferred to clips on his belt. As he pulled the box into the elevator, Noel fired a couple rounds at the survivor, who threw something in their direction. The elevator doors closed and they started up as an explosion ripped through the level behind them.

They stopped the elevator just short of the landing dock level and reloaded the semi-portable. Two guards with guns waited outside the elevator doors as they opened. They fired at pointblank range. Larry slapped one down with a mailed fist. The other backed off and then turned and ran. No one in the room was wearing armor, so Noel switched to beam power and played it around the room. Within moments only charred remains and still bodies remained. Again Larry welded the stairway door shut.

Larry unfastened the visor of his helmet and used his goggles to look around.

"Trouble coming up the freight elevator over in the main dock area," he reported. "It looks like Gil and Brandon are still in the small dock, in armor, so we'll need the semi-portable."

They loaded the semi-portable. Larry destroyed the elevator controls and they crossed the room to the passageway to the small dock. They pulled the door open and welded it shut behind themselves. The passageway had another airtight door halfway down its length. They welded it shut too.

They set up the semi-portable in the passageway in

THE MAN WITH TWO FACES

front of the door into the repair chamber. "Set?" Larry asked. Noel nodded. Larry tried to pull the airtight door open. It didn't open. For a moment they wondered what had happened.

Then Noel pointed to the gauge. "There's a vacuum on the other side."

Larry used his goggles for a couple seconds. "Cut through right there," he said, indicating a spot on the door. "You'll miss everything. Gill and Brandon are over there, and there," he said, indicating two widely divergent spots on the wall of the passageway. "We're going to have to move the semi-portable inside to be able to bring it to bear on them."

They heard a series of crashes in the passageway behind them. The first door had been burned off its hinges. Now their pursurers were trying to smash the welds loose.

Larry lifted the goggles and lowered his visor as Noel started burning through the door. It took a few moments at the range of a couple feet to get through the metal of the door and another few moments for the air of the passageway to escape. The door opened slowly. As it did they were met by a fusilade of shots. Together they picked up the semi-portable and moved it inside the chamber. Noel stumbled and fell as one of his feet was knocked out from under him by a heavy caliber slug. The semi-portable went down onto its tripod with a thump and threatened to fall over on him but Larry stopped it in time.

Noel got up again. They moved a meter more out onto the floor and then crouched behind the shields.

It took them a few moments to find their two oppo-

THE MAN WITH TWO FACES

nents and kill them. At the last moment one tried to get out to the hopper but he didn't make it to the airlock in time.

They stood up and looked around. Noel was the first to speak. "How do we move the roof?" he asked.

"I don't know yet," Larry answered. "Get into a hopper and see if it has controls for it. I'll use my goggles and see what I can find out."

It took awhile for Larry to survey the situation. "Noel, we're in trouble. We're boxed in. The crew that's after us just discovered that the rest of the passageway is in a vacuum. That's slowed them down until they can rig an airlock to get at us. Otherwise, they'll open the whole base to space.

"The roof is controlled from a central location but there is a control relay in a panel by the airlock. All we have to do is press down on the armature and the roof motors go on and it rolls back. The catch is that there are blaster batteries out there waiting for this hopper to come up so they can take a shot at it. If we stick our nose out, we're going to get it blown off. We're boxed, and we've got to have this hopper to make it back to the Bubble."

"Larry," Howard's voice came through the ultra-wave communicator. "It's worse than that. The *Boise* is exploring Alpha Centauri and they can't get back for at least another hour. The nearest regular warship is 10 hours away. Can you hold out for an hour?"

* * * *

The meeting of top officials convened in emergency session in a secure area in the pirate base. The General Agent had passed beyond anger now. He was cold, hard

THE MAN WITH TWO FACES

and calculating. He realized that he himself could well be called to account for the actions of those around the table.

"Now what excuses do you have for your actions?" he asked. His question was met by silence. "How did this McQueen escape?" Again silence. "WELL?"

"He killed two armed, experienced guards," the Base Commander finally volunteered in a meek voice.

"How? And more importantly, why did it take 15 minutes to discover the fact and sound the alarm?"

"No one was expecting trouble. We assumed that they were hung up in procedures," Norwitsky said.

"If your procedures are so sacred, why were they allowed to obtain arms, and why, *why* wasn't the communications center sealed off when the alarm was sounded?"

"Those responsible will be taken into custody and disciplined," the Base Commander said.

The General Agent snorted. "A fat lot of good that will do. What do you propose to do now?"

"The secrecy of this base has been compromised," the Base Commander said, puzzled. "Our general orders indicate we are to evacuate, destroy it and move elsewhere."

"No, it isn't that simple," the General Agent said. "Within minutes, certainly within a few hours, the Triplanetary Patrol's new supership, the *Boise*, will be here to 'neutralize' this base. I won't risk revealing the existence of our own starship, indeed risking its destruction due to your incompetence, should it get caught here in this base. This base will be evacuated after the *Boise* is destroyed, if you can destroy it. Meanwhile I, the Captain of the starship, certain specialists and certain important records, will transfer to the starship. We will await your report victory in deep space."

* * * *

"There's an old saying," Larry said, "'If you can't retreat, attack'. We were doing pretty good until we let them catch up with us.'

Noel saw a sly smile form on Larry's face. "What do you have in mind?" he asked.

Larry explained.

By the airlock they opened the control panel and Larry wedged a piece of plastic in the relay that opened the roof so that it opened and stayed open.

They opened the doors of the airlock between the dock and the repair chamber and fused the hinges so it couldn't be closed. Then they moved the semi-portable back into the passageway and started cutting holes in the metal door. The air came roaring through. The elevators inside the pirate base provided openings to all of the floors of the base. Alarms went off and a second later explosives slammed airtight doors down over all of the top level elevator openings, limiting the pressure loss to a few pounds. The doors of rooms throughout the base temporarily wouldn't open because of the pressure differential across them to the corridors. In the corridors people ran for pressure suits. Many more were temporarily trapped inside rooms.

Someone got too close to the door of the passageway to the small dock. Larry saw an arm holding a gun come through a hole and wave around a moment, until Noel switched to shells and blew it off.

THE MAN WITH TWO FACES

"This projector is getting sort of low on power," Noel reported after about two minutes. The doorway was riddled with holes. "It's got about another couple minutes' worth left."

"OK, it's time to move out,' Larry said, and produced another piece of plastic to jam the trigger.

They went back into the dock. Larry lead the way to a ladder. "This is used to get to the motors that move the roof. It won't take much to get out onto the surface, but keep down."

Larry climbed up first. He cautiously put his head out into the sunlight above the edge of the roof and looked around. When the visor darkened enough so he could see in the bright light, he saw four men in armor approaching, clumsily carrying something. Larry hooked his feet in the ladder and fumbled out a grenade from his belt. He hefted it a moment, trying to determine its weight, and from that how it would throw.

"What's up there?" Noel asked.

"Visitors."

Larry pulled the pin and, holding the trigger down, looked over the top again. Then he lobbed it. In the lesser gravity it overshot the target. He got a second grenade out and fumbled it. Noel reached out and caught it as it went past. He looked at it a moment and, seeing the pin still in place, breathed a sigh of relief. Then he put it in a clip on his belt.

Meanwhile, Larry had gotten out and lobbed a second grenade. This one went where he wanted it to go, a couple feet away from the men. The first one went off with a little puff of vapor and a cloud of material from the surface. One of the men struggling with the load

THE MAN WITH TWO FACES

dropped it to the ground. Larry saw now that it was another semi-portable. He was not injured, just knocked down by a large fragment. While he struggled to get up, the second grenade went off. The four armored men went flying like bowling pins. One landed over 20 feet away.

Larry went over the edge and started crawling toward them. Beyond them was an entrance back into the base. He was covered from the battery on one side by a knee-high ridge of rock that ran most of the way parallel to his path and from the battery on the other side by the roof of the dock. He reached the first man while still hidden from the batteries. He released the clamps on the man's helmet. It popped loose. He pulled it the rest of the way off to read the setting on his radio.

"We're in luck," he reported to Noel. "They can only see two men from the batteries. The others are out of sight. So if we stagger along, they'll assume we're the other set. That'll get us across the open spots. Their local radios are set to 2.736 MHz. I'm going to switch over there and listen for a few moments."

The band was silent. Larry listened for a full minute, then made a few noises on it as if someone was regaining consciousness.

"Who's that?" a voice asked.

Larry gave a final groan and switched back to the frequency he and Noel were using.

"If we're lucky we can fake it," he reported. "We'll play the part of a couple shaken-up soldiers, stumbling back to safety. Don't talk, groan. If you have to talk, whisper. That way they can't recognize voices." He switched over to the new frequency.

The men watching from the batteries saw an armored

THE MAN WITH TWO FACES

man half stand up and then pitch over. He whispered "Help me!" Another figure sat up slowly and half crawled, half stumbled to his aid. Supporting each other with a couple dramatic falls, and a lot of groaning they headed back to the personnel entrance to the base, where they disappeared from sight. Minutes later a third figure stood up and looked around. One of the men in a battery shot him.

Inside the entrance and out of sight of the batteries, Larry motioned to Noel to change radio frequencies.

"Boy, you're heavy," Larry said. "I thought there for a moment, when you fell on me, that I'd had it."

Noel laughed. "In a one-fourth G field? You're kidding. But now that we've made it, it seems like it was sort of fun."

"I don't think they'd appreciate an encore."

"Right!"

"OK. The first order of business is to get inside and get our hands on another semi-portable."

"How are we going to get out of here when the *Boise* comes?"

"I don't know. Maybe we can disable the whole base so there won't be a fight.

Noel didn't answer for a moment. "You shoot sort of high, don't you?"

"Somewhere around here there's a rat named Norwitsky. I owe him something."

"Bonny?"

"How did you know about that?"

"I think everyone in the Bubble knows, Larry."

Now it was Larry's turn to be silent for a moment. "Let's get moving," he said, finally. "We've got things to do. Let's go back on their regular frequency and con

THE MAN WITH TWO FACES

tinue our 'dying soldier' act. I'll be helping you off to the aid station."

They went stumbling down the spiral ramp and through the airlock into the base, expecting to find a guard on duty. When they got inside there was no one in sight except a TV camera. The room was also airless.

"Help," Larry said.

"What happened?" a voice said over the suit radio.

"A grenade," Larry whispered. "I think my arm's broken."

"The area you're in is temporarily airless. You'll have to wait until pressure is restored before you can proceed to Medical. Go to the dock 2 elevators and wait there."

Larry and Noel continued their act on the way back to the room they had recently demolished. When they got there, they both sat down along a wall and Larry motioned to switch back to their own radio channels.

"You know, they've got at least one semi-portable in there," he told Noel. "Why don't we just go borrow it from them?"

"Great idea, I feel sort of naked without one."

They switched back frequencies, got up and walked into the passageway, through the door that had been torn away and the door they had punched holes in. Their old semi-portable was still there. There was a man at the head of the passageway. Larry motioned for Noel to stay at the gun and then walked up to the other man.

"How are they coming?" he asked.

"The plastic patch should be hard in another minute or so," he said. "Then we can turn the air back on and fix the inner airlock door."

"Any idea what happened to the men we're looking for?"

THE MAN WITH TWO FACES

"They went up the ladder out of the landing dock. The battery crew got one of them and the other one seems to have run out of air and taken his helmet off."

"Who all is in the crew here?"

The man mentioned two names and motioned toward the two figures at the outer airlock. Larry nodded, and turned back to Noel, so he hid the shooting gesture he made to Noel with his thumb and forefinger.

"Any way we can recharge that semi-portable. There was no noise, since sound doesn't travel in a vacuum.

Larry ran back. They put the semi-portable on the truck, moved it to the mouth of the passageway, set it up again and walked it into the repair chamber. This time they caught the two men inside by surprise. The results were the same: both died.

To Be Concluded

50 ADVENTURES FROM NOW
Perry is pitted against the
Killer Creature

SON OF TIME VAULT

A SHOCK SHORT by WALTER (CLARK DARLTON) ERNSTING entitled THE HOUSE is what you are *supposed* to find in this space.

In that parallel world that has *got* to be better than this dyspeptic dystopia, you *did* find it here.

But in this particular spacetime continuum "The House" sprouted wings and flew away.

In other words, when the editor reached in the folder of material for #104, "The House" manuscript was nowhere to be found.

It hadn't somehow got into folder #105.

Nor even #106.

Nor several folders marked "Shock Shorts", "Future", etc.

Sabotage?

An Anti-American Action by the Antis?

Can't say.

Probably 10 minutes after the deadline—after the Final Copy for PR #104 has been expressed to the New York office—"The House" will surface. I'll find I've been sitting on it. Or my left hand mailed it to FAMOUS MONSTERS (which I also edit) while my right hand was preparing copy for PERRY RHODAN.

Anyway, I figured you wouldn't be too thrilled to find a bunch of blank pages in this issue of PR so I've selected a swell *Time Vault* tale I've been saving and this time you get 2 of 'em.

Can *you* solve the riddle of The ladder of Life?

Read—

THE MAN WITH TWO FACES

THE IMPOSSIBLE HIGHWAY
By Oscar J. Friend

*Author of "The Molecule Monsters" &
"Experiment With Destiny"*

Dr. Albert Nelson looked at his young assistant, Robert Mackensie, and scowled.

"So this was just what I needed!" he snapped. "Leave my laboratory and take a walking-tour with you in the Ozarks. Lovely vacation. Bah!"

"But, Doctor,' Mackensie protested mildly, "you need a vacation. I can't help it if we had an accident." A grin crept over his youthful face. "Besides, it's kind of funny—two erudite scientists as helpless as babes in the woods!"

But Dr. Nelson could not see the humor in the situation. They were lost—lost deep in the Ozark Mountains, their compass hopelessly smashed. And that annoyed him no end.

For Dr. Nelson was an orderly soul. He had always been a logical thinker. He had a mathematical mind that clicked like a machine. No loose ends existed for him. That was why he made such an excellent biologist. He traced everything to its source and pigeonholed it permanently within his brain before letting go of it.

To Dr. Nelson, two plus two equaled four, and he had to get that answer before he quit. Every positive had a negative, every cause an effect. There was never any unfinished research work in his laboratory, no litter

THE MAN WITH TWO FACES

of paper on his desk, no clutter of stuff in his mind. He repudiated everything which did not have a logical explanation. He had no patience with unfinished symphonies, lady-and-tiger stories, enigmas, or unsolved mysteries. Quite a definite, positive chap.

That's why he was peeved and exasperated when he and Mackensie came upon the end of the road. It wasn't the cumulative effect of the facts that they were lost, that their compass had accidentally been broken, that they had been pushing on since early morning and it was three o'clock in the afternoon now, that they were weary and scratched up and hungry and thirsty. None of this. It was the inexplicable fact of the road itself.

"What is that ahead of us?" Dr. Nelson panted as his keen eyes caught sight of a shining, white expanse through the trees and underbrush. They had been climbing steadily for the past hour, seeking a high spot from which they might survey the surrounding terrain and get their bearings. "An expanse of water, or the sky?"

Mackensie puffed on ahead. His young voice floated back in eager accents.

"It's a road, Doctor! A concrete highway! Thank God, we can find our way back to civilization now."

It was a road all right. Nelson wrinkled his brows in thought as he quickened his pace to overtake his companion. But what was a concrete road doing here in the heart of a wild country which sane white men never even trod on foot? How could there be a cement highway up here in these mountains where there weren't even county side-roads, where only wild game lived and an occasional bluejay raised his raucous voice or a lone turkey buzzard wheeled in solitary splendor overhead? And there was something else.

THE MAN WITH TWO FACES

There was nothing peculiar about the concrete slab itself. It was a quite normal specimen of the engineer's and road builder's art. Twenty feet wide, fully eight inches thick, it stretched suddenly away before the two men in a properly graded, sweet white expanse that curved through the pines and elms and cedars and dipped gracefully out of sight over the brow of a slope.

No, it wasn't the construction or condition of the road; it was the very fact of its sudden presence here. Dr. Nelson became aware of the fact that he had used the adverb "suddenly" twice in as many seconds in thinking of this thoroughfare. That described the thing. Abruptly—just like that—the road began, its near end as squarely chopped off and finished as the shoulders running along the side edges of the best behaved highways. In the midst of a primordial wilderness the road just suddenly began.

There was no evidence that it was intended to continue in his direction. No blazed trees, no surveyor's marks, no grading, no sand or gravel or lumber piles, no machinery, no tools, no barricade, no road marker, no detour sign. Nothing. Not even a dirt road, trail, or foot-path leading in any direction from the end of the concrete slab. Simply a wild and untrammeled hillside in the heart of uncharted mountains, and there, as abruptly as a pistol shot—the near end of a gleaming highway!

The incongruity of it must have finally struck Mackensie in spite of his relief, for the young biologist was standing just short of the end of the paving and staring around him in perplexity as Nelson joined him. His bright blue eyes met the steady brown eyes of the older

THE MAN WITH TWO FACES

man, and his face twisted quizzically. He wagged his hands helplessly.

"Why doesn't it go on?" he asked. "Can it be an abandoned project?"

"Whoever heard of even an abandoned trail that didn't lead at least to a house or a shack?" snorted Nelson irritably.

"Can it be a test stretch of road?" suggested Mackensie.

Wordlessly, Dr. Nelson pointed at the road's unsullied surface. There wasn't a drop of oil, a tire mark, a clump of caked dirt from a hoof, a footprint—anything, to mar the slab's virgin purity. And yet the road, beginning here in the thick of the forest, curved out of sight before them as though it led on forever, an important artery of transportation.

"It's a senseless riddle!" snapped Nelson. "And I detest riddles."

"Well, although it begins spontaneously, Doctor, it seems to lead somehwere," Mackensie said. "At least, it will lead us back to civilization. We can solve its mystery at the other end. Are you too tired to go on?"

"No. No," repeated Nelson irritably, frowning along the road. But he felt a vague reluctance to set foot on the slab. Why, he did not know. He hesitated, mopped his perspiring brow with a handkerchief, and gazed around at the deep woods through which they had come. Then he shrugged and stepped upon the end of the road.

Mackensie stepped up beside him and set off along the paving in a swinging stride. Perforce, Nelson fell in step, and they marched together in silence. For a brief space there was no sound at all save the rhythmic tramping of

THE MAN WITH TWO FACES

their boots and the occasional slithering noises which came from Nelson's knapsack. This was the little green lizard the biologist had captured some time before noon.

"Always the indefatigable scientist," Mackensie had observed when Nelson had adroitly caught the little reptile sunning itself on a rock and had popped it into an emptied sandwich box for later study.

Now, the noise of the little lizard was the only sound outside themselves which kept them company. It was the queer significance of this that caused Nelson to put his hand on Mackensie's arm and stop suddenly.

"Why are we stopping?" asked the younger man in surprise. "This beats tearing our way through brambles and underbrush by a house and farm."

"Listen," said Nelson.

Mackensie did so tensely. All around was utter silence. There wasn't even a breath of wind stirring the leaves on the trees. "I don't hear anything," he said.

"That's just it," commented Nelson. "You don't hear anything except the noise we are making. Not even the buzz of an insect—not a bird in the sky—not a rustle in the thickets alongside the road. What became of the bluejays and the gnats that kept us company and annoyed us before we reached this road?"

Mackensie's blue eyes looked startled. Nelson turned to stare along the section of road they had already traversed. It stretched there for twenty yards, white and spotless save for the faint markings of their own recent passage. It was as though they they stood alone in a dead and lifeless world. No, it wasn't like that exactly. All around them was the evidence of floral life, but a life in arrested motion. That was it—a technicolor, three-

THE MAN WITH TWO FACES

dimensional still—a rigid, frozen world in which only they themselves had the power of motion. It was uncanny.

"Not a bug crawlng across the road," whispered Mackensie in awe. "Not even a distant sound to indicate that anything or anybody is on this planet. But I have a queer sort of feeling deep inside me that—that the forces of life are surging all about us. Doctor, I feel as though this very road is quivering and teeming with life even as it lies rigid beneath our feet. What, in God's name, is all this?"

Nelson lowered his gaze to the area about his feet. Mackensie was right. There was a pyschic sort of hum or quiver to the concrete, to the very air about them, and yet everything was so still and silent. Slowly an odd impression grew upon the perturbed scientist.

It was as though his eyes penetrated the fraction of an inch below the smooth surface of the concrete slab. He felt, rather than saw, that this was an incredible highway of life, that billions and billions of living entities had trod this way before him in endless teeming throngs.

"Come on," said Nelson in a mufflled voice. "Let's go on."

It was around the next curve, where the forest thinned away and the road appeared to wind majestically across a series of plateaus on top of the world, that they came upon the first variation to the smooth progress of the road. This was a concrete pedestal about waist high on the left-hand shoulder of the highway, an integral part of the concrete itself. It was as though the road had paused and flung up a sort of pseudopodium at its edge.

On top of this slim pedestal was a cube of what appeared to be quartz glass. At least, it was crystal of some sort, faintly iridescent and sparkling under the rays of the afternoon sun. As they approached, they saw that it was a hollow cube which enclosed a powerful binocular microscope. Its twin eye-pieces, capped against the weather, protruded outside the case. On the flaring top of the pedestal, just below the glass cube and easily discernible without stooping or squinting, was a bronze plate containing raised letters. The inscription was in English.

Both men halted in amazement at the further incongruity of this. A fine microscope mounted like a museum display in a wilderness which contained only a deserted concrete highway! What did it mean?

"My God!" murmured Mackensie. "Look! Read it, Dr. Nelson."

Together they stared at the dark but clearly legible plaque.

UNIVERSAL LIFE SPORES—PAN-COSMIC
There minute cellular speciments are the tiniest evolved seeds of that phenomenon called life, whether floral or faunal, which are self-contained and practically immortal. They are propelled throughout the Universe on beams of light. Peculiarly deathless, they settle like a fungoid mold upon the most barren and arid planet and father all forms of living matter. Their primary origin is unknown.

Nelson whipped the caps from the binocular eye-pieces and glued his eyes to the lenses. He was conscious of a queer sort of magnetic thrill as he touched the glass-incased instrument. The crystal cabinet scintillated and

THE MAN WITH TWO FACES

glowed as though endowed with a life force of its own. It was impossible to adjust the controls of the microscope since they were within the glass shell but this proved needless.

On the field before his eyes, perfectly adjusted, was a typical stained glass slide similar to thousands the biologist had examined. There, immobile, deathless, changeless, were hundreds of tiny gray cells which resembled the various fern molds he had studied more than once, and yet they were different. They were cellular; they were undoubtedly bacteria—but they had a sharply distinct rim or shell which might well have been impervious to the darkness and cold and cosmic rays of outer space. Certainly Dr. Nelson had never seen their exact like before.

After a careful study he raised his head, stepped aside, and motioned Mackensie to look. The young man did so.

"Good heavens, Doctor" he murmured. "They don't even take the stain the least bit. They reject it completely standing out like dots against a field of pale pink."

"Precisely" Nelson agreed frowing thoughtfully. "And you notice that they are motionless inert—as though arrested by magic in the midst of their acivity."

"Yes," nodded Mackensie, still looking. "Doubtless they are dead."

"I wonder," said Nelson.

"I can't understand it," pursued Mackensie. "Even the most minute organisms would show at least molecular motion."

"Let's go on," said Nelson, recapping the eye-pieces. "I see another pedestal a few yards beyond, on the opposite side of this infernal road."

THE MAN WITH TWO FACES

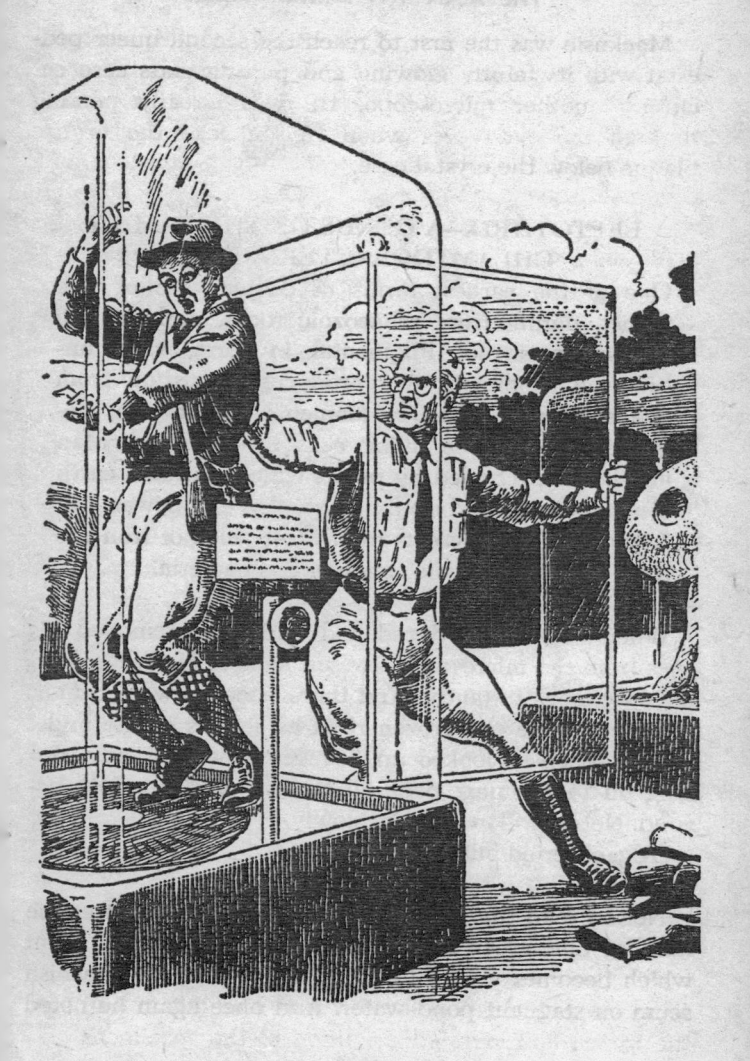

THE MAN WITH TWO FACES

Macknsie was the first to reach the second queer pedestal with its faintly glowing and pulsing glass case enclosing another microscope. He was already peering through the eye-pieces when Nelson read the bronze plaque below the crystal case.

LEPTOTHRIX—A GENUS OF THE FAMILY CHLAMYDOBACTERIACEAE

One of the earliest forms of cellular life of this planet, dating from rchaeozoic rocks, at least one billion years old. Filamental in form, with unbranched segments, it reproduces by fission from one end only. Walls of filaments are of iron, deposited around the living cells by accretion. Man and beast are fueled by plants which consume earth elements and build up by chlorophyl sun-power, but *Leptothrix* literally eats iron. Most veins of iron ore have been built by the action of this bacteria.

When Mackensie, dazed and uncertain, removed his eyes from the microscope, Nelson looked. He recognized the specimens instantly. And these bacteria were caught in an immobile net, frozen rigid as statues in the midst of life. When he looked up, Mackensie was already running on to the next pedestal twenty or thirty feet beyond. Nelson followed more slowly.

"Algae!" cried out Mackensie.

Nelson read the bronze plaque and then stared at the familiar blue-green strands of the primitive water plant which becomes visible to the naked eye as the greenish scum on stagnant pond water. And once again he noted the frozen and arrested condition of the specimens.

THE MAN WITH TWO FACES

"Plankton!" shouted Mackenzie next, reaching the fourth pedestal. "Good Lord, Doctor, this is like—like going through an open-air penny arcade of bacteriology." He smiled.

That was precisely what Nelson was thinking. He still hadn't solved the enigma of the road itself. The additional mystery of high-powered microscopes mounted here in the open in queer crystal cases he thrust to the background of his mind to be explained in due and proper course. It was, as Mackenzie said, like a laboratory of the gods. Almost fearfully Nelson looked up at the sky as though he half expected the head and shoulders of some super-scientist to materialize from behind a fleecy cloud. But nothing happened. It was still three o'clock in the afternoon. Nothing lived or moved save the two men and the confined little lizard.

One thing was significant to the Methodical Nelson as he plodded along this weird and unaccountable highway. There had been no unnecessary or haphazard placements of specimens. Everything was in logical and chronological order as far as he could determine. The trend was precisely and steadily upward in the mighty cycle of life.

Coming into view before them, lining the highway like trees in a park, were crystal specimen cases of varying sizes and shapes. No longer did a microscope accompany each exhibit. Life specimens now were in forms discernible to the naked eye. A distinct line of cleavage between plant and animal life had come into being, both being carried forward in faithful progression. And in each case every specimen was perfectly preserved and apparently lifeless. The entire array of crystal cases pulsed and glowed in the sun with an eerie life of their own.

THE MAN WITH TWO FACES

Up through the ages ran this bizarre story of life. Through the day of the fossils, the fern forests, the primordial piscine life of the sea, the first conifers, the first reptiles, the age of gigantic reptilian mammals—along the ladder of life they marched, seeing actual specimens no man, presumably, had seen before. It was like a tour through a marvelous combination of laboratory, botanical garden, aquarium, and the Smithsonian Institution.

The two biologists forgot their hunger, their thirst, their weariness. They lost all track of time, although it must have been hours and hours that they marched along this corridor of still life. It was like looking at color plates in a three-dimensional magazine of the future, or like gazing at stereopticon enlargements of the screen of life. And the sun hung brilliantly in the sky at three o'clock in the afternoon.

The written matter on the various bronze plaques—which was always there, regardless of the size of the display cabinet or the nature of its contents—would have composed a complete and unique thumbnail history of the surging course of that tenacious, fragile, but indestructible thing called life. Nelson began to regret that he had not copied down each one of them, realizing as he did so that it would have been impossible. He wouldn't have had enough paper if his knapsack had been full of nothing else.

Mackensie began to mourn that he hadn't brought a camera with him. Some of the specimens were such as man, in filling in the gaps of life's history, had never even imagined. The main enigma still unsolved, Nelson pushed onward with a mounting fever which amazed him. He felt, without analysis, that he was being drawn

THE MAN WITH TWO FACES

onward by the hand of destiny, approaching a climax, a height, a fate that was inexorable.

The same fire must have imbued Mackensie, for the young man now marveled at the Gargantuan panorama, at the magneic oddity of the crystal cases, at the puzzling thought and speculation of how this outré museum came to be, at the impossible fact that time stood still.

And then they came to the first empty display case. It was a little cabinet, and they paused to read the bronze plaque. They had long since passed into a comparatively modern era, reaching a stage of presentation which encompassed flora and fauna as it now existed. Primitive man had already appeared, and his image was in properly spaced and graded cabinets.

Nelson had got a start at his view of the first shaggy brute which was definitely the long-sought missing link between man and the lower animals. A queer and repulsive thing to the esthete, Nelson the biologist almost worshiped before the lifelike mammal. From there on the story of mankind was written graphically for the two amazed travelers to read.

But here was the first vacant case. Conscious of great annoyance, Nelson read the bronze plaque.

LACERTA VIRIDIS

This green lizard is a specimen of the small, four-legged reptile with tapering tail which, along with related families, form the sub-order of all the *Lacertilia* with the exception of geckos and chameleons, which see.

The biologist raised his eyes. But the case, pulsing and glowing with its faintly bluish-green sheen, unharmed

THE MAN WITH TWO FACES

and unbroken, was empty. There simply was nothing within it.

"That's funny," mused Mackensie aloud, as Nelson thoughtfully examined the crystal case which, in this instance resembled a bell jar. "That's the first gap in all the series."

"Yes," almost growled Nelson as he tugged at the knob of the bell jar. To his surprise, he was able to remove it. Then he saw at the base of the jar, on the flaring ledge of the pedestal, the little wheel which controlled the air-exhausting and sealing apparatus.

He accidentally placed one hand on the spot which had been covered by the bell jar, and instantly he lost all feeling in the member. It was as though his entire hand, from the wrist down, was nothing but a lamp of insensate matter. Hastily he snatched it back. At once life and feeling returned.

"What's the matter?" asked Mackensie quickly in professional interest. "Hot?"

"No," answered Nelson, replacing the bell jar carefully. "Just—nothing at all. No feeling. My hand went completely dead."

"Is it all right now?"

"Quite. There must be something about these magnetic pulsations that blanket and cut off the life force without destroying life."

"Then, if that's so, all those—those specimens we have seen are alive? Alive but dormant?"

"I wonder," said Nelson.

Mackensie shuddered silently.

"Come on," he said. "Let's go. I think I see a mountain lion yonder."

Knitting his brows in irritation at this minor break in

THE MAN WITH TWO FACES

this colossal display of specimens, Nelson followed on. The scampering, rattling, slithering, rattling, slithering sound of the little lizard in the lunchbox in his knapsack was like the annoying impulse scurrying around in his brain. They passed the chameleon, the specimens of wild game and small fauna, and reached the spot where the depicted story of this era of plant life was resumed.

Here, perhaps a couple of hundred yards on from the empty lizard case, Nelson halted in the fashion of a man who has firmly made up his mind. Mackensie looked at him in astonishment.

"Come," said Nelson. "We're going back.

"Back?" echoed the younger man incredulously. "Where? Why?"

"Only as far as the *Lacerta Viridis* case. I've got to. I've just got to. I can't go on."

"But—but, can we go—back?" whispered Mackensie.

This was a startling thought. Nelson had never considered such a possibility.

"Will we have time?" pursued his assistant biologist. "Night may overtake us as it is before we come to the end of this road.'

For answer Nelson pointed at the sun. It hung in the bright sky precisely at three o'clock position.

"Come," ordered Nelson.

Obediently, almost like a man under the power of hypnosis, Mackensie turned and started back long the highway. Nelson paced him. It was as though they breasted a strong and resistant tide, as though they fought a steady and powerful wind. Nelson felt like a man in a dream, almost overpowered with a lethargy he could not understand. Only his indomitable will forced them both onward. And still nothing moved or

THE MAN WITH TWO FACES

lived along the entire ghastly highway save the two men, walkng in the warm sunlight.

Slowly they retraced their steps and drew up before the empty lizard case.

"Well, we're here," panted Mackensie. "Now what?"

For answer Nelson removed his knapsack in a methodical fashion and took out the lunchbox. Pinioning the little lizard swiftly by the nape of the neck, he removed the bell jar and placed the squirming reptile on the pedestal.

Instantly the creature went rigid. Nelson withdrew his numbed hand and stared at the specimen. In lifelike manner the lizard rested on its four tiny feet, body half-coiled, head uplifted, beady little eyes glittering as it stared at nothing.

Primly Nelson covered it with the bell jar and turned the wheel to seal the vacuum. A faint hum resulted from within the base of the pedestal and then died into nothingness. The god of science accepting an offering. When Mackensie tried to lift the bell jar he found it immovable.

The two men stared at each other.

"At least, it is a passable specimen," observed Nelson. "It is similar to the Old World species. Let's go now."

With a quicker step he led the way. All annoyance over the empty case had vanished.

It must have been hours later, and God only knew how many curving miles, when they reached the second and final empty specimen case.

"Look!" cried Mackensie in heartfelt relief. "We are coming to the end of the road!"

Nelson had lost interest in the road. The mighty story of life which had unfolded had swept him up and on

THE MAN WITH TWO FACES

in an irresistible surge. It was with a start that he came back to a realization of his surroundings and focused his attention on the distance.

Mackensie was right. About a hundred yards on, ending in a thicket of trees on a downward slope, was the end of the road.

Just as it started, so the road ended—abruptly, inexplicably. Not far from its termination was a specimen case which appeared to be about three feet tall upon its low pedestal. But Nelson was more interested in the seven-foot case opposite him.

TWENTIETH CENTURY MAN

This specimen of the warm-blooded biped marmal with the developing brainpan and thyroidal glands represents man at the physical peak of his evolution. As has been pointed out through the various case histories, animal and plant life, having come far from a common origin, differing princpally in the matter of an atom of magnesium in chlorophyl structure instead of an atom of iron in the hemoglobin of blood, have now passed their separate evolutionary goals.

From this point on, their parallel paths converge, finally uniting once more in a common structure which approaches the apex of mental development.

Dr. Nelson raised his eyes from the bronze plaque. The pulsating hollow cube was empty. There was no specimen. Instead, there was only a door of beveled glass which swung out over the road on invisible hinges, as if inviting a weary sojourner to enter and rest—for eternity.

THE MAN WITH TWO FACES

The biologist frowned in utter exasperation. Why, of all specimen cases, should this one be empty? He pulled restlessly at one ear as he turned to stare along the road. He was annoyed again, disappointed, to note there were no more specimen cases save the one three-foot case at the very end of the way.

The story was almost told. Past hundreds of thousands of crystal cases they had walked for endless hours—only to find this most important case, as far as mankind was concerned, empty. Somehow, Nelson could not go on and leave it thus. His methodical nature seemed to be driving him onward with inexorable logic. His gaze fell upon his companion.

"Mackensie," he said in a queer voice. "Mackensie, come here."

The younger man paled and shrank away.

"No," he cried out, intuitively guessing the other's purpose. "No! You are mad, Doctor. Let's get away from this hellish thing. I—"

He ended in a cry of stark terror as Nelson pounced upon him. The biologist was twenty years older than Mackensie, but he was also the larger man physically. Mackensie had no chance against him. The struggle was as short as its meaning was horrible. In a matter of seconds Nelson had his victim helpless.

"No!" screamed Mackensie, horror dawning in his eyes. "Dr. Nelson, you mustn't!—You can't do this! You—"

He ended in shrill scream after scream of fainting madness as Nelson lifted him erect and carried him to the ajar door of the crystal cabinet.

"It is painless," murmured Nelson gently. "I know. *And why is the case empty*, if not for one of us? Answer me that!"

THE MAN WITH TWO FACES

But Mackensie was past answering anything. He was passing into a state of cataleptic horror.

Like a man in a dream, like a puppet controlled by extra-terrestrial strings, Nelson shifted his burden dexteriously around to face him and then, balancing himself carefully, he thrust the body of his companion squarely and smoothly into the empty crystal case. The change that took place was miraculous, instantaneous. The texture of Mackensie's body became like marble. Remaining erect, he rocked back against the rear of the cabinet and then forward like a tottering statue.

Nelson quickly pulled he heavy crystal door around, literally closing it in the set face of his companion. With a soft *whoosh* of air, the beveled edges of the door fitted smoothly into the beveled crystal frame—and the last case had its perfect specimen.

The biologist was trembling as he stared into the glazed eyes of his former laboratory assistant. Then he signed, mopped his brow, and glanced at the sun. It was three o'clock in the afternoon.

Turning slowly, as though loath to part company with the man who had made this incredible journey with him, Nelson strode on to the end of the road.

Reaching that last case, he paused to study the specimen within. Almost in the shade of the thickening trees, the pulsating aura of the cast was faintly phosphorescent. But it was the nature of the specimen that fascinated the biologist.

Squat, scarcely three feet tall, pallid and sickly brownish in tinge, the thing looked more like an overgrown mushroom than anything else. A mushroom with a bulging dome that was a horrible caricature of a human head. A pair of enormous orifices denoted what may have been meant for eyes. The mouth was nothing but a seam or a weal which indicated where a mouth once had been. The thing was sexless and stood upon three rootlike feet. At last Nelson brought himself to read the bronze plaque.

THRYOIDICUS—PLANT MAN

The final evolution of mammalian life upon this planet. Composed principally of a fibrous brain tissue and a free iodine producing organism which is the development of what was formerly man's iodine plant, thyroid gland located in the throat, this creature has neither blood nor chlorophyl.
Like *Leptothrix*, this form of life has learned at long last to assimiliate its food directly from the elements, transmuting it instantly and releasing free energy. *Thyroidicus*, the ultimate goal of physical evolution, is practically all brain. The next step in the stage of evolution, inevitably, crosses the boundary of animate existence, and life becomes purely spiritual.

That was all. The story was told. The end of the road was reached—abruptly. No blazed trees, no surveyor's marks, no grading, no material piles, no machinery, no tools no barricades, no detour sign. Not even a dirt road, a trail, or a foot-path leading in any direction from the end of the concrete slab.

Simply a wild and untrammeled hillside in the heart of uncharted mountains, and the road which had begun as suddenly as a pistol shot led nowhere and ended as precipitately.

THE MAN WITH TWO FACES

Dr. Nelson was a methodical and orderly soul. Ironically so, he realized grimly. He hadn't been able to help himself. His cold logic had been tapped to the nth degree.

He thoughtfully turned and stared back along the way he had come. He felt that vague and incomprehensible tremble of vibrant life flowing onward in the road beneath his feet. Now there was not an empty case, not a broken thread in the two lines of specimen cases which stretched off into the limitable distance there. The record was complete.

THE PERRYSCOPE

MIKE MARTIN, 3843 Los Padres Rd., Santa Maria / CA 93454, seconds the notion of a Hugo for PERRY.

Dear Forry & Wendayne Ackerpeople;
I have never written to the Perryscope before, but the increasing quality of recent magabooks has pushed me to the typewriter to try. In general, the PR series beats all that I've read previously. If you prevent the spelling and typographical errors, (a whole line was printed upside-down in PR#96! See the fourth line, page 126) a Hugo should be within your reach. The editorials and puns are good, and Wendayne's translations are superb. The future slanguage is well done and the potential and outlook of PR's future is bright. Is there an upcoming weekly publication of PR? I hope so. And when will the rumors of an Atlan series become a reality? Congrats on a happy 1st 100 Perry's and may you print 700 more! May the great bird of the galazy never roost in your Ackermansion. Here's a buck toward the payment of the SON OF ACKERMANSION! I challenge all self-respecting Rhofans in every corner of Terra and Arkon to do the same. (EVERY RHOFAN! ! ! !)

THE MAN WITH TWO FACES

KAREN E. WEBER, POB 311, Mt. McKinley / AK 99755 gives an Alaskan cold shoulder to those in the "Lower 48" who are icy toward Future Slang.

Dear 4E Ackerperson,

Despite the great delay involved in communicating with the Perryscope, I am determined to answer the query you posed in PR #94 about the slanguage you have developed for PR.

I approve, wholeheartedly.

As a college graduate who majored in Journalism and minored in English and who has always had an intense interest in the history and linguistics of the English language, I feel that I have some slight background in the field to give my approval a bit of weight.

English has always used contractions, corruptions, acronyms, affixes and numerous other devices to enrich and expand its vocabulary. To expect that process to stop in the 21st Century would be akin to be expecting Pucky to give up carrots. It just won't happen.

In just the few, the very few, years since I was a teenager, "groovy" has become obsolete and "out of sight" has gone out of mind.

There are only three solutions to the slang problem. One, the series characters can use 20th century slang; but that wouldn't be realistic. Two, the series can forego slang entirely and merely use standard English. This would be acceptable, though it would make the characters seem rather dull and stuffy and would still be basically unrealistic since slanguage has been around as long as language has. The third solution, and the one that gets my vote, is to let you, Forry, continue creating.

Reggie and Pucky would not be the same without your

THE MAN WITH TWO FACES

"silly" slang and your "corny" dialog and I like them just the way they are, thank you.

The only change I'd suggest making is leave out the footnotes. They are distracting and unnecessary. You can tell what a slang expression means from the context and, generally, you can also tell what it derived from. Glord, most of them are obvious.

I would, however, like footnotes on the Arkonide and Interkosmo phrases. I never can remember what "forvala" & "shantel" & "gova dorani" & "Karandi" mean.

As for you fellow readers who disapprove of Forry's style of slang. Why don't you send him a few suggestions for improving his 21st century slang vocabulary; but don't ask him to cut it out entirely.

As for me, I say "All the way with Forrest J." Slots out, Forry!

MARTIN WALLACE, 78 Allison Dr., Moncton, N.B., Canada E1E 2T8 expresses a few opinions:

Perry himself is a great man and a wonderful character, but I get tired of hearing him losing and gaining his self-control. Reginald Bell is the best companion for Perry. Even though he talks a lot and spreads gloom and doom, he actually is the best-controlled of them all. He lets his tension out by talking instead of keeping it bottled up inside him in the name of self-control.

John Marshall's mutants are great and Pucky is the greatest! A mutant with a sense of humor is wonderful. Pucky is so powerful and so human, whoops! Excuse me! I meant to say: Pucky is so powerful and so mousebeaver too!

THE MAN WITH TWO FACES

ANDY ANDRUSCHAK is back from 6933 N. Rosemead (Apt. 31), San Gabriel / CA 91775, with brief remarks on non-Rhodanic material:

Glad to see an end of the Coblentz serial. It was ok for the first few chapters but degenerated into cheap pulp fiction toward the end. No more of this author, please.

As for Cummings, rah!

TONY TURLEY, Rt. 9 Box 803, Anniston/AL 30201, obviously believes in FIAWOL (Fandom Is A Way Of Life).

Forrest J. Ackerman & Wendayne

I have read your work on Scifi for many years, and I must say that I think that you're both the greatest. I have some questions about Scifi that I hope you can answer. Where is the Ackerman Museum located? And what does it hold? Does it have the entire PR collection? How many PR's are there in English & German?

I've made Scifi my life. I've given up girls for it. When girls ask me why I quit them, I just say that I find Scifi more exciting. They laugh in my face, but I don't care.

I have 98 PERRY RHODANS, 85 Doc Savage, 36 Avenger, 15 Shadow, 7 Tarzan, 6 Star Trek, "Scifi Hall of Fame", "Mote in God's Eye", "Logan's Run" (it's great), Books by Asimov, Doc Smith and Farmer, a "Planet of the Apes" book and 500 or 600 comics. I guess that ends my book collection and will give you an idea of what I like.

(The Ackermuseum is located at 2495 Glendower Ave., Hollywood/CA 90027, holds approximately 200,000

books, magazines, paintings, movie props, manuscripts, records, Tapes, etc., including the 800 German PERRY RHODAN magazines, German ATLAN series, etc.)

LONGTIME RHOFAN MILTON STREETER writes from "Somewhere in the Mediterranean":

Many numbers ago, you suggested that the readers present anecdotes in the lives of Perry, Reg, etc. The lastime I saw one was in number 60, and I wish to contribute one of my own now.

Reg has a peculiar sense of humor (remember the interlude at Ellert's Crypt in Book #4?), and I suspect that like me, he's prone to some godawful puns. With this in mind, I present: "The Miracle," and I accept responsibility for the groans it may cause. (*Watch out for this in a future issue.*—FJA)

"The Spaceships of Rhodan" at Rhodan 1 only made me want to see more. I do hope the publishers will see fit to release such an edition—I'm starting to lose my perspective in relation to the *Drusus!* And when we get to the *other* dreadnoughts in future adventures, I may die of shock *without* such diagrams!

Also, place my vote for publishing the Missing 3 Episodes, perhaps the most famous books never printed!

Wendayne and Associates, thank you; the translations are a joy to read.

Thanks again very much for the hours of enjoyment you've given me, here in the ocean and back home.

Perry's just got his second wind now—we'll get that Hugo yet!

(Yes, the same person who wrote from Athens 4 years ago!)

PUT ON A HAPPY FACE!

DON'T wear that other face—that one of disappointment, despair, doom, because you got to the newsstand too late and the new PERRY RHODAN was sold out.

Wear the smile of confidence, secure in the knowledge that YOUR copies of PR will appear each month at your place via hyjump from Hollywood.

Wear the contented face of a SUBSCRIBER!

A foresighted Rhofan who has sent in $8.95 for the next 6 numbers or $17.95 for the next 12.

A subscriber in Japan sent $100 to get his copies airmail!

Similarly a Rhofan in Australia.

But for as little as $8.95 you can have peace of mind for the next 3 months. Or 6 months assurance of receiving RHODAN for $17.95.

NB: These subscription rates only good during the month of issuance and until the next price change (if any). Check the *current* issue to see what the going rate is if you pick this up when it's a back number.

Send CHECK or MONEY ORDER (leaving back of either blank). CANADIANS, please send POSTAL MONEY ORDERS ONLY, payable in U.S. DOLLARS. PERRY RHODAN #105 thru. . . . .

```
KRIS DARKON
2495 Glendower Ave.
Hollywood/CA 90027
```

NAME (Print Clearly) ....

(AGE) ....

ST. ADDRESS, POB or RFD ....

CITY ....

STATE (Spell Out) ....

ZIP ....

COUNTRY ....

PERRY RHODAN SPACE CENTERS

ALABAMA

WATKINS BOOK SHOP
9168 Parkway East
Birmingham, Ala. 35206

PROFESSOR BOOK CENTER
2901 18th St. South
Homewood, Ala. 35209

CALIFORNIA

GARDEN GROVE BOOK SHOP
12926 Main St.
Garden Grove, Calif. 92640

READMORE
120 East Avenue J
Lancaster, Calif. 93534

THE GOLDEN QUESTION BOOKSHOP
2218 Mac Arthur Blvd.
Oakland, Calif. 94602

DISTRICT OF COLUMBIA

UNIVERSAL NEWSSTAND
735 14th St. N.W.
Washington, D.C.

FLORIDA

O'HENRY'S UNIVERSITY BOOKSTORE
5406 Stirling Rd.
Davie, Fla. 33314

KANSAS

RECTOR'S BOOK STORES INC.
206 East Douglas
Wichita, Kansas 67202

MASSACHUSETTS

SIGHT & SOUND, INC.
173 Cambridge St.
Boston, Mass. 02114

DUNHAM MALL BOOK SHOP
31 Dunham Mall
Pittsfield, Mass. 01201

MINNESOTA

PAGE ONE BOOKSHOP
712 Laurel St.
Brainerd, Minn. 56401

NEW JERSEY

FAIR HAVEN BOOK STORE
759 River Road
Fair Haven, N.J. 07701

GALLERY EAST BOOKSTORE
103 Third Ave.
Neptune City Shopping Center
Neptune City, N.J. 07753

PASSAIC BOOK CENTER
594 Main Avenue
Passaic, N.J. 07055

NEW YORK

COLLINS STATIONERY
124 West Post Road
White Plains, N.Y. 10606

NORTH CAROLINA

D.J.'s NEWSCENTER
North Hills Mall
Raleigh, N.C. 27612

D.J.'s COLLEGE BOOK & NEWS
2416 Hillsborough St.
Raleigh, N.C. 27607

D.J.'s NEWS & BOOK
Crabtree Valley Mall
Raleigh, N.C. 27612

OHIO

KAY'S BOOK & MAG. SUPERMARKET
620 Prospect Avenue
Cleveland, Ohio 44115

NEWS DEPOT
358 High St.
Hamilton, Ohio 45011

GOLDEN TRIANGLE BOOK STORE
516 S. Locust St. (Tollgate Mall)
Oxford, Ohio 45056

OKLAHOMA

RECTOR'S BOOK STORE INC.
4813 N. May Ave.
Oklahoma City, Okla. 73112

OREGON

THE BOOK VAULT
3125 S.W. Cedar Hills Blvd.
Beaverton, Ore. 97005

THE BOOK VAULT
3rd & Main
Hillsboro, Ore. 97123

THE GALLERY BOOKSTORE
220 Liberty N.E.
Salem, Ore. 97301

THE LOOKING GLASS BOOKSTORE
421 S. W. Taylor St.
Portland, Oregon, 97204

SOUTH DAKOTA

COVER TO COVER
Brookings Mall
Brookings, S. Dakota

TEXAS

COCHRAN'S BOOKSTORE
4521 WestGate Blvd
Austin, Texas 78745

UNIVERSITY CO-OP
2246 Guadalupe
Austin, Texas 78705

BOOKS N THINGS
314 Cove Terrace S/Ctr.
Copperas Cove, Texas 76522

THE BOOK STORE
9348 Dyer
El Paso, Texas 79924

THE BOOK STORE
6003 Mesa
El Paso, Tx. 79912

THE BOOK STORE
9518 Viscount
El Paso, Tx. 79925

ACE NEWS
8180 Main St.
Houston, Texas 77025

BELLAIRE NEWS
5807 Bellaire Blvd.
Houston, Texas 77036

BOOK DEN on RICE BLVD.
2510 Rice Blvd.
Houston, Texas 77005

TEXAS

GUYS NEWS
3622 Main St.
Houston, Texas 77002

ALAMO BOOK STORE #21
North Star Mall
San Antonio, Texas 78228

ALAMO BOOK STORE #11
214 Central Park Mall
San Antonio, Texas 78216

ALAMO BOOK STORE #10
175 Valley Hi Mall
San Antonio, Texas 78227

ALAMO BOOK STORE #14
McCreless Mall
San Antonio, Texas 78223

ALAMO BOOK STORE #8
Wonderland Mall
San Antonio, Texas 78201

ALAMO BOOK STORE #7
503 East Houston
San Antonio, Texas 78205

UTAH

BY'S MAGAZINE SHOP
Main Street
Salt Lake City, Utah, 84119

WASHINGTON

GIBSON HOUSE, INC.
109 N. Tower
Centralia, Wash. 98531

WISCONSIN

BOOK WORLD
30 South Main
Janesville, Wisc. 53545

CANADA

BAKKA BOOKSTORE
282 to 286 Queen St. W.
Toronto, M5V 2A1
Ontario, Canada

PERRY RHODAN

Just $1.25 each

#81	Pucky's Greatest Hour Brand
#82	Atlan in Danger Brand
#83	Ernst Ellert Returns Darlton
#84	Secret Mission: Moluk Voltz
#85	Enemy in the Dark Mahr
#86	Blazing Sun Darlton
#87	The Starless Realm Darlton
#88	Mystery of the Ant Scheer
#89	Power's Price Brand
#90	Unleashed Powers Brand
#91	Friend to Mankind Voltz
#92	Target Star Scheer
#93	Vagabond of Space Darlton
#94	Action: Division Three Mahr
#95	Plasma Monster Mahr
#96	Horn: Green Voltz
#97	Phantom Flat Darlton
#98	Idol from Passa Mahr
#99	Blue System Scheer
#100	Desert of Death Mahr

Available wherever paperbacks are sold or use this coupon.

ace books, (Dept. MM) Box 576, Times Square Station
New York, N.Y. 10036

Please send me titles checked above.

I enclose $.................. Add 35c handling fee per copy.

Name ....

Address ....

City.................. State............. Zip........